Adulting Life Skills for Teen Girls

How to Master the Most Essential Skills in Life And Become a Strong And Independent Woman Without Anxiety And Self-Doubt. How to Make Friends, Manage Money.

Amora K. Rose

Please consult a licensed professional before attempting any techniques outlined in this book.

By reading this document, the reader agrees that under no circumstances is the author responsible for any losses, direct or indirect, that are incurred as a result of the use of the information contained within this document, including, but not limited to, errors, omissions, or inaccuracies.

Table of Contents

Amora K. Rose

Your Free Gift!

Hey there! I just wanted to express my gratitude for buying my book. As a token of appreciation, I would love to offer you my books and a Guided Meditation Audio completely for FREE!

It's my way of saying thank you for your support, and I truly hope it helps you in your journey.

To Download The Free
GIFTS Scan The QR Code
or Go To:
obiez.com/lsg-gift

Anxiety Relief Guide

- How Anxiety Creeps Up and How to avoid it
- 4 Practical Tools to Empowering yourself to handle your Emotions
- A Simple but Extremely Effective Technique to Treat Panic Attacks
- Little known Secret to Be Socially Fearless
- And Much More

The Power² Of Gratitude For Teens

- The Secret To Gratitude in Teens
- 5 Ways Gratitude Can Exponentiate a Teens Life
- How a Simple Action Can Improve Your Family's Relationship
- And Much More

To Download The Free GIFTS Scan The QR Code or Go To:
obiez.com/lsg-gift

Join Our Advance Reader Group

GET OUR NEXT BOOK FOR FREE

Go to: obiez.com/lsg-gift

Or Scan the QR Code

Introduction

You've gotten this book, looked at the cover, and I'm guessing it is exactly what you were expecting. Whether you're on the verge of facing the big world by yourself or your parents are trying to help you find your independence, hopefully this book eliminates the need for any awkward conversations that neither you nor your parents want to have in person.

Do you know why your home or personal space need to be optimized? Do you know how to stock your kitchen and pantry? Do you know how to change a tire? These are basic life skills that you need to know, and, unfortunately, you can't always call mom and dad to help you with the little things. But that's alright, because even though you may be rolling your eyes at the fact that you have to read this book, I pretty much guarantee your independence.

Let's be honest, there is a life you envision for yourself. Maybe you see yourself as a book author or editor living in the big city, going out with friends whenever you'd like. Maybe you see yourself as a diligent college student who can use their time as they wish, not being accountable to anyone. Maybe you see yourself in a corporate job running an organization.

Imagining this future life for yourself is great, but it isn't all about the fun and easy times. The life you envision for yourself comes with hard work and almost endless responsibilities.

Now, I'm not trying to say this as a way to scare you off or to deter you from the life you imagine. All I'm saying is the good parts of independence also come with the hard parts. It's up to you to make sure you choose the best outcome for yourself.

You may be wondering how I could be imparting valuable life skills to you, even through a book. Well, I have some street cred. Okay, not necessarily street cred, but I know some things.

For starters, I am a woman myself. I know what it's like for the world to look at you in shock and awe when you roll up your sleeves and change your flat tire in a skirt and heels. Nothing beats the satisfaction of asking someone to back away because *you got this*.

Next, assuming you're a teen or in your early 20s, I have been around people your age for most of my life as a teacher and as a counselor. Heck, I have even been your age once before, but a lady never tells her age.

I want to provide you with the opportunity to have the much needed life skills in your artillery that will allow you to thrive, whether you need these skills or not. There is an old saying that you rather have it and not need it than need it and not have it, and that saying has never been more true than when you needed to change a light bulb… by yourself… in the dark.

So whether your folks are trying to help you as you venture into a new part of your life or whether you need the help to be more prepared, this book will hopefully serve as a guidebook to teach you the skills you need and to have them in your mind ready to use or to pass on to someone else who may need it.

How to Use This Book

Without further ado, welcome to your all-inclusive guide on adulting. I know, no one wants to think about adulting until the time comes. But the time doesn't usually get announced—it just sort of creeps up on you. One day you wake up, and mom and dad are no longer two doors down the hall from your bedroom for you to ask them if the Wi-Fi is working. Nope, you have to check if the Wi-Fi is down all by yourself.

Whether you are nervous, afraid, or embarrassed to ask certain questions or whether you feel that your folks may just not understand, it's alright, but it certainly doesn't mean that you have to face this world by yourself.

This book will cover important aspects about garnering certain life skills. You will learn about domestic skills that are required for you to take care of a home and that will allow your home to take care of you. From basic laundry and maintenance, making easy meals, and taking care of your vehicle and sticking to maintenance plans, you will be equipped to take on the independence of living by yourself, whether you are headed off to college or getting your own apartment.

Next, you will learn how to effectively use social skills that will help you in public spaces, in professional spaces, in relationships, and with friends and family. An important part of social skills is staying safe when you are alone and being alert of your environment.

This book will teach you important things that not even your parents knew at this age. You will learn about financial well-being, taking care of your mental and physical health, and nurturing your own personal development.

Yes, this may seem overwhelming, but I hope to provide you with enough information that can help you be successful in understanding each of the topics in this book. This book is the starting point of your adventure into life. Everyone always says that the scariest part of doing something new is taking the first step. This will hopefully serve as a handbook for those first steps. You can then venture further with the confidence needed for self-exploration and learning what the world has to offer without fear.

Now, let us take this first step together. Let's develop the skills needed to take on the world!

Chapter 1: Domestic Skills

Whether you are heading off to college or you're still in high school living with your folks, there are certain things that you need to do to make a space your own. Whether it is the small space of your bedroom or the larger space of an apartment, an important part of making a space your own entails keeping it well-maintained. This means learning some basic household and organizational skills that won't only make your space comfortable for guests, but it will also make you feel like a better version of yourself.

In this chapter, we will look at:

- how to get yourself and your space organized.

- how to develop an effective routine, not just for your daily life, but even for care and maintenance of yourself and your home.

- how to take care of different parts of your home, including the chores that come with it.

- how to take care of a vehicle, if you have one.

Organizing Your Home and Your Life

Organization is an extremely important part of everyday life. I'm sure you have gotten frustrated with your parents more often than you care to admit with them always being on your case about cleaning and tidying your room. But the reason behind that is that as long as your space occupies their space, they want it to look and feel a certain way. When you make a space entirely your own, you can find things easily and you can function better.

Why Organization Is Important

For a better understanding of this concept, let's look at what organization is and why it is important. It is your home, and in your personal space, being organized means knowing where everything is and making sure that your home is a place that both you and others would like to occupy. Being organized also helps you clear your mind (which is pretty great when you have an exam or assignment coming up—no more procrastination), it helps you clear out things that you don't need, and it helps you find things easily.

Organizing Different Parts of Your Space or Home

The first and most important part of organizing your home, whether you are just starting the process or doing some upkeep, is to declutter. It can be hard to let go of certain things in your space, especially if your best friend gave it to you or if you bought it with your own money. But I have a system that I use to declutter my space: I ask myself if I have used the item in the last month, three months, or year. Then I ask myself if I am probably going to use it in the next month, three months, or year. Depending on the answer, I either toss it or donate it to charity with a firm reminder in my mind that if a need for that specific item arises later on, I can head down to the store and get one.

Next, you want to remember that there is no such thing as being "over-organized." Get the sticky notes, dig out the label maker, and get the Sharpies because you are about to go overboard, and that's fine.

When you are organizing different parts of your space, you are going to need to approach it in specific ways. The way you organize your bedroom will differ from the way you manage your bathroom and kitchen. Also, depending on the stage you're at in life, you may be in a dorm that has no kitchen or an apartment that has much smaller spaces and less room for *stuff*. It's important to adapt your organization according to your space.

Let us look at some ways that you can organize different spaces.

Kitchen

As you venture off into the world of independence, you will find that the kitchen space doesn't just belong to your mom. You can make it your own, and even if you share a kitchen with your mom, you can still cook dinner for the family without disrupting the existing flow of the space while still making it comfortable for you.

1. Organizing any space isn't something you can do before you head out for a movie, so make sure you have enough time set aside to start and finish the task.

2. Start working in specific areas of your kitchen. If you are working in the pantry, clear out the entire pantry and organize it entirely. If you are organizing your fridge, empty it out completely and organize it entirely. This way, you will have multiple organized spaces instead of one large space that is only halfway organized.

3. Decluttering is something you need to do consistently. If you have any duplicated items, like two whisks, you might want to consider giving one away.

4. Ideally, you want to be able to see everything you have in your kitchen, whether it is utensils or spices. This can be easily achieved by using containers to store all items and properly labeling everything.

5. In the kitchen, it is best to keep similar items together. Try to avoid storing crockery (cups and plates) with ingredients.

6. When packing away pots and pans, always keep in mind that heavier things are best stored lower and lighter

things go up higher. The last thing you'd want is to have a pot ding you on the head or have a top drawer collapse under the weight.

7. Using containers, dividers, organizers, and labels is effective in cabinets and in drawers for keeping things organized. They also help with the previous point of making sure you can see everything that is in the drawer or cabinet. Now, you don't need to have a label maker, but having some sticky notes on hand will be a great help because you'd be surprised at how many brown spices exist!

8. Try to optimize counter surfaces and the way you pack your cabinets and drawers. This means that first, you'd want to keep counter space as clear as possible. If you must have items on the counter, it should only be the bare minimum and it should be items that are used on a daily basis. In your cabinets and drawers, try to keep the most used items front and center so you don't waste time searching for them.

Living Space

Whether you have the delightful chore of taking care of the lounge area at your parents' home or you spend most of your time in your room with the door shut, headphones on, or the TV playing, you need to keep your living space well organized.

A living space refers to the general area within your home that you occupy. This means that broom cupboards and closets aren't living spaces, but the lounge, dining room, kitchen, and your bedroom are living spaces.

1. Have a decent storage unit in the space, whether it is shelves or a cabinet. This allows you to pack away any items that are not in use while still having a fixed space to keep these items (such as board games, books, magazines, and even TV remotes).

2. Allow your space to be adaptable and fluid. If you are entertaining guests or having friends over, your living room or living space need to adapt. Having a daily decluttering or organizing strategy will make sure that the buildup of cups, plates, and board games doesn't overwhelm you.

3. Always clean up after yourself and guests. The last thing you would want is to clear away day-old snacks from the night before.

4. Adding some shelves to a living space is really multifunctional because not only can you store everyday items in the shelves, but it is also fixed in one space,

meaning that it doesn't shrink your living space by taking up any room on the floor.

5. Optimizing your coffee table is a game changer in any living room. As the anchor of the room, it needs to be functional for you to place a cup of coffee or a book, but you don't want to overclutter it. Adding large decorative items like a bowl or vase will reduce the buildup of clutter while still leaving you with some functional space.

Bedroom and Closet

This is probably the most important area in your home and the most important personal space that you occupy because this is the place where you go to rest, where you find your greatest comfort, and which is entirely your own.

1. Declutter all the spaces in your room, including your nightstand and tables. If you don't use it on a daily basis and it isn't a source of light, it can probably be packed away or even tossed.

2. Make your bed every day. Not only will it make the room appear less cluttered, but it is also much easier to hop into after a long day without having to first tidy your bed or risk getting poked by a pen.

3. There's no point having a decluttered bedroom only to have a closet that is bursting at the seams with a mess of clothes and other items that you have no control over. There are a few steps you can take to organize your closet:

    a. The first thing you can do is clear out the clothes that you no longer use. You can donate clothes that you have outgrown, that are no longer in style, or that are no longer *your* style.

    b. Organizing your closet by season will also make it easier for you to keep track of the clothing items and shoes you own. We have all been there where we have forgotten about clothing items we have purchased and they live their days out hidden at the back of our closet. Seasonal organization makes sure that winter items and summer items are always up-to-date, all year long.

    c. Take some time to decide what clothing items will be folded, what will be hung up, and what will go into drawers. Then you can invest in the hangers, storage containers, and drawers that you may need.

d. As tedious as it may sound, it is important to keep track of what clothing items you have. This may help you hoard fewer items. If you haven't used a pair of jeans or an outfit in three months or a year (depending on what time limit you give yourself), you can definitely donate that item.

e. If you are rotating your clothes by season, you're going to need to get some extra storage to keep the out-of-season items until they are needed. For winter items, you could possibly vacuum seal sweaters and you can use large containers for summer items.

f. Lastly, having a dedicated space for formal wear is a great way of knowing what to wear when a special event arises and making sure delicate items don't get damaged.

Part of organizing means maintaining the spaces around you. The last thing you'd want is to start organizing from scratch after a few months because you didn't maintain your efforts from the first time. Trust me, maintaining your space is better than starting from scratch.

To maintain your organization, here's what you can do:

1. Keep surfaces clean and tidy. It's easy for a space to appear cluttered when there are papers or random items scattered around.

2. Actively avoid hoarding items. I have told myself many times that I am going to keep something because I may need it later and I never ended up using it. Don't fall into the same trap.

3. After every use, put items back where they belong. This is especially helpful with laundry!

4. Lastly, there is no right or wrong way to organize a space. If you have the basics in order, such as decluttering your space, grouping similar items together, and labeling everything, the way you set up and streamline your space is entirely up to you. Remember, your aesthetic needs to shine through and a room needs to be functional and fit for *your* purpose.

Keeping Important Things Safe

A big part of keeping your space organized is knowing where to find not just anything, but *important* things. Your home is your safe space, and it is also the space where you keep important items safe. These items could be spare keys, important documents, and special jewelry items that have a high value to you.

Before we look at how you can organize and keep documents and valuables, let us look at what documents and items should be prioritized:

- identity documents: Items such as birth certificates, are extremely important and sensitive, so while you do need them for very specific functions, it could be disastrous if they landed in the wrong hands.

- Social Security cards: Keep cards or documents with your Social Security Number on them in a safe place and memorize the number.

- passport: If you have one, keep it secure. It is extremely important for international travel and can take time and money to replace.

- financial or bank documents: These letters and bank communications could have sensitive information on it such as your account number or even your address.

- tax information.

- legal documents, property-related documents, and lease information or signed contracts.

- any sensitive health-related information and documents.

- vehicle ownership papers.

- all instruction manuals, guarantees, and warranties on all appliances and machinery you may have.

Once you have all your documents together, you can begin sorting or organizing them in plastic files or sleeves. This will keep the documents safe and allow you to group similar documents together. For example, in one part of the file, you can group all identity-related documentation, such as your birth certificate, your Social Security details, and your passport together.

Next, you can group all medical documents together, all legal documents together, and all appliance-related documents together.

You can also store documents in chronological order or in order of importance. This means that documents you are more likely to use can be kept front and center, and older documents that you may not need but are important for record purposes or because they contain sensitive information can be kept at the bottom of the pile.

Once you have your personal and important documents organized, it is time to put them in a safe place where it is not easily accessible to others, but you can easily access it when you need it.

Here are the best ways to store these important documents:

1. You need to get an appropriate storage container. In many cases, important documents are only issued once. You want to store them in a way that doesn't make them susceptible to water or insect damage.

2. Next, you want to make sure that you have copies and backups available of all your documentation. Copies of documents are often accepted at some places in place of the originals, and it is a great way to make sure that the originals don't get misplaced.

3. Possible storage solutions for important documents include having a small storage cabinet that has a lock system, a lock box, or even an at-home safe.

4. You may want to get a box that is large enough to contain your important documents as well as other valuable items, such as spare keys, money, expensive jewelry, and any other sentimental items or items that are important to you.

The Importance Of Routines

Routine is a great way for most people to thrive. Don't get me wrong, routine is not the absence of spontaneity, but rather, it is about keeping yourself healthy and functional so that when spontaneity does come along, your life isn't derailed.

But, what is a routine and why is it important? Many people think that a routine is doing the same thing over and over again, each day, and not deviating from these daily tasks. And while this is true to some extent, it actually goes much deeper than that.

A routine is the structure of daily tasks and activities that generally follows the most logical pattern (Skilled at Life, 2016). It is how you form the habits that are necessary for you to be successful in life. Whether you have goals set, planning to ace an exam, or hoping to succeed in a specific activity, you need to add practice time into your daily routine so you can achieve your goals and find success.

Having a routine can help you get the most out of your 24 hours in the day. It also helps you manage your stress, have greater quality sleep, and even be healthier overall, especially when you develop beneficial habits as part of your routine.

But how do you create an effective daily routine? There is no blueprint or one-size-fits-all way of developing a routine because everyone has unique needs, tasks that need to be fulfilled, and priorities that are important to them alone. Here is how you can create your personalized daily routine that best accommodates your unique tasks:

1. Make a detailed list of everything you need to do in the day. This list can be extremely detailed, including menial

tasks such brushing your teeth and having a bath or shower. You can even make two lists: one of the important tasks that need to be completed and one of the menial tasks that are a necessity.

2. Next, you're going to want to structure your day. When do you find yourself to be most productive? Do you have any time at school or college to do any tasks? If not, you want to make sure that you don't set any tasks in your routine to happen during that time.

3. You can decide how specific you want to be. You can set time aside, for example 7:00 a.m. to 7:45 a.m. for your morning shower, brushing your teeth, doing your hair and getting dressed, and you can break this time up into smaller increments for each task. Or you could just set this time aside for daily hygiene and grooming. As long as you only do this for general daily tasks and not specific tasks which, if you are not detailed enough, may lead you to forget.

4. Now you are ready to organize your tasks and times into your routine. Sorting your tasks out by deadline, priority, and the length of time it will take to complete each task will allow you to get the most value out of your time. You can then slot each task into your routine, making

sure to schedule harder tasks during the time of day that you're most productive.

5. Now it's time to try out your new routine. Write down your routine and put it somewhere that you can see it, or you could even make use of a digital or online organizational tool. You may not get it right the first time, and you may find yourself giving too much or too little time to a single task, but that's alright. Take some time to adjust your routine, and before you know it, your routine will become a habit and you won't even need to use your written reminder.

Tips for sticking to your new routine:

- Be realistic with yourself and with your time. You'll probably be setting yourself up for failure if you give yourself 30 minutes to complete a task that actually takes 45 minutes. You'll also likely end up wasting time or getting distracted on social media if you give yourself 30 minutes to complete a task that takes only 15 minutes. Also, you can't do all your tasks in one day. Some things need to be scheduled for tomorrow.

- Be flexible and allow yourself some space for the unplanned. Yes, having a routine is great for organization and for relieving stress but allow some flexibility for a cup of coffee with a friend or a movie date. This will also help make sure you don't get bored with the tasks on your to-do list.

- Schedule easier tasks for times of the day when you don't really feel like doing anything. That way you're still productive, even when you don't feel active, and it won't feel stressful because they're easy tasks.

- Set daily goals about what you're hoping to achieve in the day and reward yourself when you accomplish those goals. This will give you the motivation to keep working through your routine, even when you don't feel like doing it.

- Monitor how much progress you make. This will allow you to better adjust your schedule if need be.

- Prepare yourself for failure, success, boredom, and superseding the goals you have set for yourself. These are all parts of life, and you need to be prepared that your daily routine may or may not lead to exactly what you're hoping for.

Creating and Using a To-Do List

You may have read about a to-do list in the previous section, but you may not be entirely sure about what it is. And since it is such a fundamental and important part of forming a healthy routine, here is how you can create an effective to-do list:

1. With so many digital planning and organization applications available, you may wonder what is the best medium for your to-do list. This comes down to personal preference, and maybe because I am "old school," I prefer a good old-fashioned pen and paper.

2. It's always good to know exactly what it is you need to do for the day. If you don't know what tasks you need to do, there isn't a way to create a to-do list.

3. Generally, you're going to make a note of everything you need to complete before organizing them into priorities.

4. Remember, you are working with tasks, not goals. How much of a task you are hoping to complete or accomplish will depend on your routine organization later on.

5. Make a note of which tasks occur each day and set a special time to complete those tasks.

6. Then, you're going to create your to-do list prioritizing the most important tasks, which are usually the ones that are looming or the ones you have been avoiding because they are harder.

7. Once you have them on paper or in your digital organizer, it's time to start working your way through the to-do list.

8. The last items on your to-do list are tasks that aren't urgent and that you could probably leave for the next day if you run out of time to get through your list. And while this isn't recommended, it is a great option to have.

Scheduling, and Why It's Important

Another important element of creating a daily routine is scheduling. Scheduling is attributing a dedicated amount of time to a specific task. Just in the same way that you would schedule an appointment to see a doctor or dentist, you should also set aside specific times for tasks in your day. This allows you to better meet deadlines, make progress, and be accountable to yourself and others if need be.

Taking Care of the Home

Have you ever looked at your mom and wondered how she just knew things? Whether she knew what to buy at the store or how she just knew how to do things in the kitchen and around the house, somehow moms have a way of gliding through the house effortlessly and finding all the missing items that you and your family seem to lose.

Well, your mom may have had a very good teacher, or she may have been thrown into the deep end and had to figure things out by herself and create a space and routine in which she thrived.

Lucky for you, I'm here to give you some pointers on how to navigate your own space as well as your mom does while still giving you the freedom to make it your own. After all, there is no set rule on how to function and run your home space.

Kitchen

Grocery and Pantry

Stocking up your pantry on grocery items can be tricky, especially when you don't know what you need. It's not about heading into the store and taking one of each item. That is neither feasible nor realistic. Instead, there is an effective way to stock your pantry from scratch while still making sure you have the basics.

Before you actually go out to the store to stock up your pantry, there are a few things you need to know:

- Have a plan in place. Decide what you are hoping to eat for the next week or two and make a rough meal plan. It doesn't need to be perfect, nor does it need to be set in stone, but it will allow you to form a baseline of the general grocery items that are a staple for every meal (such as salt, pepper, garlic, other spices, and rice to name a few).

- Buy items that you can make multiple meals from. Whether it is soup today and stir fry two days from now, if you can use similar ingredients in both meals, it will make shopping much easier. We are going for ease and less waste rather than variety and throwing out multiple ingredients that may have gone bad.

- Last, make a list. Have you ever seen a grown-up do shopping without a list? The last thing you want is to head back to the store after unpacking everything at home because you realize you forgot one of your staple items. Having a list will also allow you to keep track of what items are running low when you go shopping again.

When you go grocery shopping to stock up your pantry, always remember that expensive doesn't always mean the product is the best quality. Here are steps you can follow to get the best food items without breaking the bank (Michaels, 2020):

1. It may be tempting to want to stock every bare cupboard in your home, but sometimes, the best thing you can do is buy enough groceries just for the next week or two. When you go to stock up, you will probably have some

ingredients at home making each subsequent trip to the store even cheaper.

2. Always compare prices. There is a common notion that if something is more expensive, it must be a better quality. But this isn't always the case for one of two reasons: 1) items that may have been more expensive might be on sale, or 2) the more expensive item isn't a better quality but it is just attached to a well-known brand. For this reason, it is always best for you to compare prices before tossing the most expensive item into your shopping cart.

3. Buying items in bulk can be a major money saver. To know for sure, compare the unit price, which is usually printed on the shelf price tag. Often you will save more for larger quantities. In many instances, if the store at which you're shopping does sell items in bulk, it may be a great idea to buy nonperishable items this way, especially when you notice a sale. This, coupled with shopping the sales, will make sure you save a pretty penny.

4. Have you ever seen a store-brand item and immediately skipped over it because you don't know how good it would be? Well, if you're shopping at the store, it must be pretty good. In many cases, unless it's a sale on

branded items, the store brand will be cheaper. It may be a great idea to shop the store brands for savings and they often have a money-back guarantee if you don't like them as well as the name brand item.

5. Whenever you go shopping, one of the best ways to avoid overspending or overbuying is to make a list and stick to it as closely as possible. Yes, you may want to add a candy bar or orange juice to your cart, but the majority of the items you purchase should be items that you actually need. Avoid these "impulse buys."

6. When you are at the store, look and compare prices. Most of the expensive goods are placed at eye level because stores take advantage of the fact that customers don't search for bargains. Cheaper items may be placed higher up or lower down, so don't take the first item your eyes land on.

Must-Have Pantry Items

Among the fresh produce that you may buy, there are some must-haves that you can consistently stock your pantry with that allow you to have an almost endless variety of meals.

These constant or common items that can be used in multiple dishes are as follows:

- **herbs and spices**: Life is too short to eat flavorless food. Make sure you have salt, sugar, cinnamon, cumin, paprika, chili powder, vinegar, and onion and garlic powder, along with some dried herbs, such as parsley, rosemary, and thyme. You can mix and match these in any meal to bring about different flavors.

- **dry ingredients**: Pasta is an extremely versatile dish, as are most starch-based meals. Whether you are cooking a meal or baking, there are some staples that you can stock your pantry with such as flour, baking powder, yeast, cocoa powder, rolled oats, popcorn, rice, pastas (whichever pasta you enjoy eating or cooking the most), and cereal.

- **canned goods**: Being extremely versatile with a longer shelf life, canned goods can add dimension to any meal without you buying fresh produce and risking that produce going bad. You can get a variety of canned goods such as tomatoes, corn, beans, peas, and tomato paste or puree.

- **meat and fresh vegetables**: Aside from fresh fruit and vegetables, if you are a meat, chicken, or fish eater, you will need to add a few of these items to your shopping list. However, you're probably going to want to stick to items you actually use or actually like. There's no point buying carrots if you don't eat carrots. In addition to fruit, vegetables, and meat items, add milk, cheese, frozen veggies, and other condiments to your list.

Once you familiarize yourself with your kitchen space and your pantry and you learn what meals you tend to prefer making for yourself, you can begin stocking up and adding repeat items to your list.

These items include

- Peanut butter or other nut butters, if you are not allergic, are a favorite staple food.

- Crackers have a longer shelf life than bread, so they make a good option for something to keep on hand. If you tend to consume bread without it going moldy or if you like making sandwiches, then you can skip the crackers and stay stocked up on fresh bread as and when you need it.

- Cereal can really be an all day food, especially if you are not particularly hungry. Adding a few varieties of cereals to your pantry can be extremely beneficial because it allows you to switch things up if you feel like having cereal for breakfast and lunch.

- Canned items are staple pantry items that you just can't go wrong with. They have long shelf lives and are really versatile.

A great idea is to also plan a menu for each week, every two weeks, or for the whole month. This takes the guesswork out of what meals you need to cook, and it also helps you keep your grocery list quite consistent.

Cooking Tips

Now that you have your kitchen and your pantry stocked, it's time to get to cooking. When it comes to actually creating a meal, it is easy to follow a recipe step-by-step. But as you become more comfortable in the kitchen, you may find yourself adapting recipes to suit your taste. For example, if you prefer spicy food, you may change up the amount of spices added to a dish, or you may add your favorite flavors and spices to a recipe that doesn't necessarily require them.

The starting point of creating any meal is safety. After all, you will be working with a hot stove, hot oils, and other obvious dangers like knives. Here are some safety tips that you should always follow when you're cooking:

- The first and seemingly most obvious tip is to wash your hands before and in between handling different food items. While this may seem obvious, you'd be surprised how often people forget this. Wash your hands before touching food because of germs. Next, avoid cross contamination by washing your hands between handling meat items, vegetables, and fruits. The same goes for the utensils you are using with each type of food.

- Learn how to use a knife. The last thing you want is to have your finger on the wrong side of a kitchen knife. Use a claw hold on food items to prevent the tips of your fingers from coming into contact with the sharp side of a knife's blade.

- Have the tools needed to put out a fire, whether it is a fire extinguisher, water (for a nonelectrical fire), or sand in the instances where water cannot be used. Remember, fires can come from cooking on an open gas stove, baking in an oven, or from food burning in a pot.

- Always turn pan and pot handles away from you because you don't want to bump the handles and send hot food flying all over the place or have small children trying to grab them.

- Clean up as you go as this will prevent buildup on hot plates that could ignite.

- When it comes to cooking various types of food, there are different concepts to consider. For example, if you are cooking chicken, be sure to wash your hands and utensils because raw chicken can have salmonella. It is also great to separate vegetable items and meat items when you're cooking or preparing a dish as well.

- Lastly, steam is often as hot as fire. Be careful when you open a pot or stir one because the steam can burn you.

Essential Recipes

Knowing how to cook a few good meals can take you a long way in your meal planning. Also, when you can swap out ingredients, such as chicken for beef, you know you have a versatile dish.

Rice

This is generally one of the easiest things you will make because the instructions are also clearly listed on the packaging. But you will first start by measuring out the amount of rice you hope to make. Usually, rice expands when it is cooked, so don't overfill the pot. Additionally, you can cook rice to serve as a side dish for one meal, or you could spice it up, add in some chives, and have it as a meal on its own.

Salad

A salad is a great way to incorporate a wide variety of ingredients together for a meal. Maybe you have a bad taste left in your mouth because a salad just reminds you of a bland, lettuce-based meal that has no flavor and keeps you hungry all day. But that doesn't have to be the case.

Spruce up your salad by adding in some nuts or some herbs such as parsley or coriander. This will add flavor, color, and texture to the salad. Toss in some chicken, and you have a great-tasting and filling meal.

Meat

When you prepare some form of meat item, whether it is steak or chicken, you want to make sure that you bring them to room temperature before cooking to ensure the best result. Also have all the vegetables, spices, and other ingredients you may need to make the dish prepared before you start cooking.

All meat items have different cooking times, but it is important to cook the meat to perfection and, especially, to ensure that chicken is always fully cooked for safety. There are also different methods that you can use to cook meat, chicken, and fish which include frying, grilling, roasting and preparing it with other vegetables in the form of a stew or curry.

Spaghetti

Much like rice, spaghetti is a variety of pasta that is extremely diverse. However, other pastas, such as penne, tagliatelle, or good old-fashioned macaroni, are also great and versatile, but I notice that most people tend to use the same pasta often owing to personal preference.

To cook any form of pasta, you will generally follow the instructions on the box, but for the most part, you would set some water to boil with a lot of salt. Thereafter, you're going to add the pasta to the pot and boil it for about eight minutes, or about one minute less than it says on the packaging. This is because you want your pasta to be *al dente,* or a little firm, and if you are cooking it to accompany bolognaise or a creamy chicken and mushroom sauce, the pasta is going to continue cooking when you add it to the sauce.

An important tip to note when it comes to any kind of food is that you should try to minimize food waste as much as possible. If you are living on your own, I know it can be extremely tricky to just cook for one person, but if you do find yourself with leftovers, pack them away and you may not need to cook for one day in the week when you can have leftovers instead.

Just be sure to store all leftover foods in airtight containers in the fridge or in the freezer to prevent them from going bad.

Keeping Your Home Clean

At some point, you have probably heard how hard it is to maintain the cleanliness of a home and how frustrating laundry is to do. But allow me to let you in on a secret… The only reason why people may complain about the cleaning chores is because they haven't found a consistent and streamlined way of maintaining their home yet.

The greatest hack you will ever learn is maintaining what has already been cleaned and keeping your space organized, which has already been discussed earlier in the chapter.

Some tips for keeping your home clean include

- Set aside one day twice a month to do a full clean. This will mean cleaning the inside of your home from top to bottom.

- Once every three months, clean the outside of your home thoroughly, which includes cleaning the windows. Also have your gutters cleaned seasonally after leaves fall.

- On a daily basis, wipe down surfaces and any spills or leaks and dedicate two days a week to sweeping, vacuuming, or mopping the floors in your home.

Keeping your home consistently clean each day reduces the amount of excessive work that needs to be done. This means that instead of doing a big cleanup job every weekend when you should be resting or having fun with friends and family, you are dedicating a few minutes each day to ensuring that your home stays tidy.

Laundry

Part of keeping your home and yourself tidy is making sure you get the hang of doing laundry. In many cases, people use washing machines or they even head over to the laundromat to have the clothes washed and dried. Gone are the days of hand-washing clothes. Even washing machines have delicate hand-wash settings for clothing items that require a gentler touch or extra care.

Here are some tips that will make your laundry days much easier, whether you're doing laundry at home or in a communal area:

- Before you even get to the laundry machine, your clothes need to be sorted into delicates, colors, and whites. In general, deep, rich, and dark colors can be washed together, although all new items of clothing should be washed in a load of similar colors because the dye of most new items will run the most in the first two to three washes.

- Sorting your clothing items will not only allow you to adjust the general setting on the washing machine for those particular items (such as using a gentle or hand-wash setting for delicate garments and underwear), but it will also help you to create smaller loads, which are more efficient when doing laundry. I know you're probably worried about doing more loads as you may use more water, but washing machines are designed to adjust the water use for the amount of clothes in the load. It also helps the clothes get cleaned more effectively as they move around easier in the machine during the cycle.

- When it comes to detergent and fabric softener, remember that a little goes a long way. If you are one person and you find yourself running out of detergent before your next trip to the store, chances are, you are using too much.

- A great way to minimize ironing your clothing items is to remove them from a dryer as soon as they are done drying. Once you remove them, it is best to fold them and pack them away or hang them up immediately because this will avoid wrinkles in your clothes.

- An ironing tip that I have found to come in handy is that it's easier to add five minutes to your dressing time to allow for you to iron the outfit you are going to wear than it is to set two hours of your week aside to iron all of your laundry, even if you won't be wearing it for the next week or two.

The best advice that you will ever hear when it comes to laundry is that you should avoid procrastination at all costs. It needs to be done, and it can't be avoided. If you are one person, you can do laundry once or twice a week. Set aside this time in the week and plan accordingly. The best thing about folding laundry is that you can watch TV while doing so.

Fixing and Maintenance

When there is some handy work that needs to be done around the house, it is easy to "call a guy," especially when that guy is your dad and he is in the next room. But if you are out of the nest, living on your own, or need to get some handiwork done and your dad isn't home, it is great to know that you can do it without assistance from anyone else.

When you think about your dad or anyone else doing some maintenance work or fixing work or even hanging up a picture frame, what's the first thing that comes to mind? A toolbox. For the basic needs that you may have, you won't need an elaborate toolbox filled with all the tools that the mind can imagine. Instead, you will need some basics that can be effectively used in multiple conditions.

You will need

- a set of screwdrivers, which will include Phillips and flathead screwdrivers of a few different sizes;

- hammer and nails;

- wrenches of different sizes to help you loosen or tighten pipes that may be leaky;

- heavy-duty tape;

- pliers;

- heavy-duty scissors.

If you are hoping to do any handiwork yourself, it is not necessary to have power tools unless you are certain you know how to use them. For the most part, having these basic tools will enable you to temporarily pause the faulty function of certain parts in your home until you can call maintenance for help.

Gas, Energy, and Water

Every home has utilities such as gas, energy, and water, and it is important, for financial and safety reasons, that these services and equipment are well-maintained and taken care of. Granted, because these are often linked to local and state entities, there may not be much that you can do on your side to fix a major problem, and you will have to place a call at your local gas, energy, or water department.

However, there are things that you can do at home to make sure that your utilities are functioning the way they should be:

1. You need to check your bill closely. Familiarize yourself with it to understand what each section means. This will

assist you in knowing whether you have a leak or whether you need to call in professional maintenance services.

2. Understand what your average usage is. You won't know if you are spending too much on water or if you have a leak if you don't have a baseline from which to work. Over three months, monitor your average usage and compare your use with neighbors or those around you whose home is similar in size to yours and who has about the same number of people living in that home.

3. If you hear or see drips or leaks, investigate them or, if they are severe, turn off your water at the main valve. If you smell a strong odor of rotten eggs, this could be a gas leak. Shut off your gas at the mains. This will be especially beneficial while you fix the leak or while you wait for professionals to assist.

4. Whenever you make any electrical changes or adjustments, even if you're just changing a light bulb, be sure to turn the power off at the circuit breaker. Before turning the power off, make sure you have all the tools and equipment you will need so that you aren't searching for tools in the dark and so that you aren't turning your main power switch on and off unnecessarily.

Disaster Management and Prevention

If we were always prepared for an eventual disaster, it wouldn't come as a surprise or a shock to us when it happened. But we live in a world where the weather, power supply, and other crises are usually unpredictable. In these cases, it is always best to prepare for any disaster than be caught off guard and unprepared.

Flood Management and Preparation

Floods can occur in your home from natural disasters or from burst pipes or water tanks. While pipes or hot water heaters can be repaired within a day, natural disasters don't have a time limit on them, and the best you can do in the case of these disasters is to be prepared.

The first thing you need to do is familiarize yourself with the area in which you are staying. Is it known for heavy rainfall and extreme floods or adverse weather conditions? If so, your home and community will usually be built in a way that prepares you for such disasters.

1. While weather is often unpredictable, there are people who dedicate their lives and their careers to monitoring weather patterns and unexpected changes, and they usually work together with local authorities to warn citizens and communities of an impending disaster. It is

important to listen to these warnings and take the appropriate precautions.

2. Make sure you have enough supplies to last you in case you cannot make it to a store for a few days. These supplies include nonperishable food supplies, water, candles, and first aid items.

3. Have an emergency pack made up of flashlights, medications, a cell phone charger, and bottled water.

4. You may be wondering why you need flashlights and nonperishable foods. Well, you can't really use electricity in a flood because it is well-known that electricity and water don't go well together. This also means that your refrigerator and freezer may not work, and you will need to elevate all your electrical appliances.

5. Take special precaution to protect valuable items that you hope not to lose in potential flooding, and take precautions to keep all important documents safe.

6. You can flood-proof as much of your home as possible by elevating as many electrical components and furniture to prevent as much damage as possible.

Power Outage

There are many things that could cause a power outage, and even if you are entirely off your country's utilities grid, you may still face instances where there are area-wide power outages. This can be caused by a number of factors.

1. When the power goes out, the first thing you should do is assess if it is localized to your home only or if your entire area has been affected. If it is just your home facing an issue, then it may mean that you need to check your circuit breaker or make sure that you have stayed on top of your utility payments.

2. The next thing you should do is make sure that everything that needs power is charged and that your fridge and freezer remains closed so as to prevent any cold air from escaping.

3. Next, you want to disconnect your appliances, laptops, and TVs from their main power source to prevent any appliance damage from any power surge that may occur when the power does come back on.

4. If it is a planned power outage, you can try to plan ahead and prepare meals for when you are out of power. However, if it is an unexpected power outage, you may need to put plans in place to prepare meals that don't require electricity. You could make sandwiches or cook on gas if you have the equipment to safely do so. This is also a great way to heat small batches of water if need be.

Taking Care of Your Vehicle

One of the greatest joys of growing up is that you gain your independence. One of the most tangible ways that people pinpoint as a moment they were considered "grown up" is the day they get their driver's license.

Getting Your License

Getting a car and your license are two monumental occasions, and they don't only mark your independence but also the responsibility that you pursue when you take ownership of a vehicle. Whether you have saved up and paid for your own vehicle or your parents have given you the most phenomenal gift ever, it lies with you to make sure that your car is well-maintained and looked after.

As exciting as it is, getting your actual driver's license is the last of a long list of steps that you need to take that may cause you anxiety and stress, but it is a once-off deal, meaning that once you are qualified to drive on the road, you are qualified for life. It is, however, important to know that there are different state regulations that may affect the process in getting your license. However, the general process you may follow is:

- Get your learner's permit. This is the first step that will ultimately get you behind the wheel successfully, and while you don't physically get behind the wheel at this point of the process, it does familiarize you with the important rules of the road and safety procedures. It also gets some legal aspects out of the way (such as attaching a legal permit to your name).

- Once you have your learner's permit in hand, which will usually come after you have passed a written test, the fun begins, and you can officially and legally get behind the wheel of a car to learn how to drive.

- It is then time to either find a driving instructor or ask someone to teach you how to drive. This practical learning, coupled with studying your driver's handbook, will equip you for both the theoretical aspect of your license examination as well as the practical aspect.

- Going for your license isn't as simple as showing up when you have a gap in your calendar. You'll need to make an appointment, take the appropriate documentation with you (this would include your ID, your learner's permit, and any other state-required documentation), as well as the fee you are required to pay to take your test, and then you can take the written or theoretical part of your driver's test. Then, you go out on the road with an examiner.

- Depending on your skill and the outcome based on the examiner's test, you will either pass your license test or you will need a certain period of time to lapse before you're allowed to retake the test.

Going for your license exam can cause you a lot of anxiety and even driving can cause extreme forms of anxiety (Richards, 2022), but it is important to know that the reason these rigorous tests are in place is because road safety is of paramount importance. Being safe on the road is not only important for you but also for all other road users, which include drivers, cyclists, and pedestrians.

Vehicle Maintenance

To get the most life span out of your car, you need to do regular and thorough maintenance. This will save you a lot of money in the long run and keep your car running optimally. Because cars are exposed to the elements like rain and sun and because they move at high speeds and you need to brake often, they tend to go through a lot of wear and tear.

There are a few things that you can do in terms of preventative maintenance that make your vehicle life span a lot longer. These include taking care of different elements of your car:

- What's the first thing you look at when you get a new appliance or you need to set up a new piece of furniture? You look at the instruction manual. While you have covered the basics of driving in your license test, the functionality of your car will be detailed in your car's manual. It will not only tell you what buttons control which functions, but it will also give you a guide on when your car should go for certain maintenance services and what fluids need to be changed at specific intervals. As a tip, the amount of maintenance will directly correlate to how much you use your car. If you find yourself not using your car as often, you may perform maintenance on your car after longer intervals.

- Filling your gas tank is a common task. On your dashboard, there will be a clear indication of how much gas remains in your car and a light will appear when your gas is running low. Additionally, your instruction manual will tell you what type of gas you need to fill in your car.

- When you do take your car for regular maintenance, be sure to insist on an oil change if it falls into the appropriate intervals. Also, make sure that the company doing your maintenance provides you with a detailed invoice and breakdown of what they have done.

- When it comes to your tires and brakes, they need to be properly maintained for safety purposes. You should also make sure that you have a spare wheel so that you can change your wheel in the case of a puncture.

- o Before you change your tire, you should make sure that you are safely on the side of the road.

- o Then, you need to turn your hazard lights on. To stay safe, it is important that you can see others and they can see you.

- o Next, you need to remove all necessary tools from the trunk of your car along with the spare wheel.

- o Before jacking your car up, you need to make sure your car's handbrake is engaged. Then loosen all the nuts that hold your wheel tightly in place.

- o Then, you can jack your car up, remove all the nuts, and remove the flat wheel.

- o Next, you will put the spare wheel in its place, tighten all the nuts, lower the jack, and finish tightening all the nuts completely.

- When it comes to your windshield, you want to make sure that your wipers are in proper working condition meaning that they clear all water from your windshield effectively. Additionally, fill enough wiper fluid under the hood of the car to optimize your visibility. You also want to inspect your windshield for any cracks or chips.

Remember that a small chip can grow and eventually turn into a big crack.

- Headlights always need to be in working order. Every two to three months, you should have a friend with you to check all front and rear lights. They will stand outside your vehicle while you turn all the lights on and off to check their functionality.

- Keeping your car clean and taking it for a wash every one to two weeks is also highly recommended. Not only does it add to the aesthetic appeal of your car, but it also enhances safety by making sure you are clearly seen and that your lights aren't covered in dirt.

Accidents

In life, there are many adversities that you and others will face. Some of these challenges are avoidable, and others aren't. One such unavoidable one is car accidents. If you do find yourself with the misfortune of experiencing a car accident, there are a few things that you need to do (Brill & Rinaldi, n.d.):

1. Immediately after the accident has occurred, you need to check your physical condition. If you have been severely injured, it would affect your ability to perform any subsequent tasks in this list. However, if you are able to, you can follow the next steps.

2. Next, you need to stay at the scene of the accident.

3. Then, you need to call any emergency services that may be required at the scene, including police, ambulance, or firefighters.

4. Thereafter, it is time to exchange details with all those involved in the accident as well as witnesses that were around the scene. You're also going to need to document the incident in detail, taking pictures and videos of the scene from all angles for your insurance company.

5. If your car is not in a safe driving condition, contact a tow truck to have it taken to your mechanic.

6. Lastly, if you are injured or feel any discomfort even hours later, head to the doctor or emergency room to be checked out.

It may seem like growing up and adulting takes up so much time and effort. However, once you form a routine of home care and car care, everything will fit seamlessly into your lifestyle. And while you may never or rarely encounter any disasters, it is always best to be prepared.

Instead of feeling overwhelmed by the information presented to you, you can rest assured that you are the person many will come to if they find themselves in a pickle.

Part of being a well-rounded person and having the much-needed adult skills to thrive as an independent individual means far more than just knowing how to take care of a home and car. It also means that you have appropriate social skills that will allow you to thrive and adapt in almost any social interaction. Let's delve deeper into the world of social interactions and how you can thrive in your social life.

Chapter 2: Social Skills

We human beings are social beings. We come into the world as the result of others' actions. We survive here in dependence on others. Whether we like it or not, there is hardly a moment of our lives when we do not benefit from others' activities. –Dalai Lama

No matter what your personality type is, one of the beautiful and wonderfully unique aspects of being human is that we are innately social beings.

I'm sure you have found yourself thinking that you could probably do just fine by yourself. Maybe your parents annoy you or you had a fight with your best friend and discovered it was quite easy and enjoyable to be by yourself curled up in your room. And while you thought that you could do that forever, the reality is that humans thrive on interactions with other people. Even if it is a smile with someone who works at the store, these small encounters and interactions are important for our mental, emotional, and social well-being.

Many people mark their personality type up to whether or not they enjoy socializing with others, but the reality is that this doesn't impact whether or not you need social interactions but rather how you engage in them. There are two personality types that you may have heard of or that people talk about often: introverts and extroverts. While it is commonly assumed that these are two concepts that lie on opposite ends of a scale, it is not quite as black-and-white. It is more like a spectrum with some people having stronger introvert or extrovert traits than others.

While introverts are more inward-facing and may be quieter and more perceptive of their own feelings, extroverts appear more social, thrive in an environment with many people, and are highly perceptive of others' feelings. However, both introverts and extroverts need social interactions. Extroverts may prefer larger groups, whereas introverts may prefer smaller interactions or engaging one-on-one (Raypole, 2019).

Additionally, there are those who possess traits from both these personality types whereby they feel more extroverted some days and more introverted other days, or they feel extroverted, but they need some time alone and by themselves to revive their social battery. But neither type are isolated beings and both need social interactions.

Communication Is Key

At the basis of our social interactions exists communication. It is the foundation on which we build relationships. Without communication, not only do personal relationships come crashing down, but so do many aspects of society.

You have probably seen the importance of communication in your own life, in a school context, personal context, or even within your family. You may have even seen firsthand how so many things fall apart when people don't communicate. There may be times where you find yourself annoyed by what you have said, or you're convinced you have put your metaphorical foot in your mouth and spend hours thinking back on how you could have given a better response to a specific interaction.

This is how you can become an effective communicator in almost any environment:

- There's an age-old rule about not saying anything if you don't have anything "nice" to say. To build on this notion, being an effective communicator essentially means not saying anything that isn't necessary.

- Read the context and the space of the room before communicating. This will give you cues on whether you should communicate in an informal or formal way, what may be appropriate or inappropriate to say, and who you should be engaging and talking to.

- Be honest in your communication, be clear in your communication, and remember that hidden meanings never work in any situation.

- Communication is a two-way interaction, and part of communicating effectively means listening. But it's also important to remember that communication doesn't just happen verbally, but it also happens in the written medium and in the digital space. It would be wise for you to effectively communicate in all mediums.

- It is never okay to "ghost" anyone, in any context. Always respond to someone whether it is in person, over email, or even text, unless the conversation has come to a natural stopping point. A good and effective communicator will know when they have reached this stopping point.

- Don't speak just for the sake of saying something. It is better to have an objective that you hope to achieve with your words rather than merely tossing out strings of sentences that don't contribute value to the interaction.

- Part of being a good communicator is knowing what *not* to say. If the opportunity for silence presents itself, take it, and if you don't have an opinion or knowledge on a certain topic, that is alright too—no one expects everyone to know everything.

Now that you have communication down to a tee, it is time to build relationships on this firm foundation.

Relationships

While this isn't a how-to guide on dating, romantic relationships are an important part and interaction in life. Whether you have already started dating, or much like getting your driver's license, it makes you too nervous to consider, eventually a time and situation will present itself when dating starts crossing your mind. But relationships in the context of this book go far beyond that of romantic relationships and, rather, encompasses all relationships you may encounter in your life, including friends, family, and, yes, potential romantic partners.

It is important that I mention that the categories of relationships that one may encounter in their life is not always clear-cut, and you will see this more and more clearly as you grow up. In school, you had your best friends and your "other" friends, all of whom were close to you. But as you grow older, the dynamics of your relationships shift, and you may discover yourself finding it hard to have a best friend. Instead, you may have friends that are important for different reasons in your life, such as at work or for leisure time.

Nevertheless, forming and developing relationships remain important at every stage of life you may find yourself in.

Building Relationships

You will build different relationships with a variety of people in your life that will ultimately reflect the environment in which you engage and interact with them. For example, the relationship you have with your parents may not be the appropriate relationship to form with your boss.

While there are many ways to develop long-lasting relationships in the personal, professional, and familial spheres, there are a few common threads that you will encounter and that you can use no matter what type of relationship you are forming with someone (Deutschendorf, 2015).

1. We have already established the importance of communication, but one of the best ways you can form a relationship with a person is to actively listen to what they say to you. Additionally, take note of the person as a whole—their body language and other nonverbal cues will give you unspoken messages and tell you how they feel about different topics.

2. What may be important to you may not be important to someone else, but showing someone that you care if they care goes a long way in forming a relationship with

them. Ask after the people that matter to them, ask about the things they appear to be concerned about, and show an interest in things they seem interested about. It will go a long way.

3. Forming a relationship with anyone takes work. No relationship is self-sufficient. It requires you to make time, make an effort, make a phone call, or send a text. Yes, these mediums of communication are two-way avenues, and both parties need to make the effort.

4. In line with putting in the work to grow and develop a relationship, always make sure that you put in the effort consistently. Life is busy, and people will understand if you aren't calling them every single day. But at least set time aside once a week or even once every two weeks to give someone your undivided attention.

5. With relationships being a give and take, you can't expect someone to share what is held close to their heart when you don't share what is close to your heart, too. While you may not want to share your life story and deepest secrets early in a relationship, as the relationship develops and progresses and as you feel more comfortable, let people in as much as you would like to be let into their lives.

6. Lastly, don't bond over the temporary social aspects of life. When you are out partying and you meet a friend, you will be able to tell if this is a friend that only seems to be around when you're out or if they are a friend you will speak to when you are at home doing nothing.

Making a Good First Impression

Before you can build a relationship with anyone or decide that this is a person you hope to build a relationship with, you both need to make a good first impression on each other. This will determine if this is just a first and last interaction or if this is someone you would really like to get to know. Once again, first impressions will differ depending on the context in which the first meeting is taking place. It is also important to know that it's okay to make a good first impression and not want to interact with that person again. It's also okay to not care about the type of impression you are leaving on someone, as long as you remember that this will ultimately contribute to the mark and reputation you leave behind in this world.

Remember that you're not going to be everyone's cup of tea, and that's alright because some people like coffee more anyway.

The first impression you make in a professional space will be different to the one you make on new potential friends or on a first date. If you are heading into a professional space, the best way to make a good impression is to be punctual to whatever the interaction is (interview or meeting), dress appropriately, acknowledge and enforce the appropriate formalities (like shaking hands), and be friendly yet professional (smile and engage in small talk if necessary while exuding confidence).

In a social space, whether it is with friends or a potential romantic partner, you can make a great first impression by being friendly, having a positive outlook, engaging in active conversation, making eye contact with people, and being entirely yourself. You don't want to create a false first impression by allowing people to think you're anyone but yourself.

Being the social creatures that we are, we need to engage with different people for different reasons. As you grow up and your life changes from being in school to heading off to work and college, to settling down in marriage, the people you have in your life will differ greatly. But now that you know how to start or begin forming these relationships, let's get to the fun part: the different types of relationships in your life and how to nurture each one.

Friends

Some people may say that friends aren't everything. But those people have probably never seen your friends pick you up when you felt like you were at your lowest. There are two important facets of having friends: making new friends and nurturing and keeping your old friends. Each of these takes its own unique set of work, and it is important to remember that given the complexities of social interactions, making new friends may never mean replacing your old friends.

Making New Friends

Making new friends can be tricky because you ultimately need to decide if you even want to make new friends. Making friends can be easy if you remain kind, outgoing, and positive to those you interact with.

There are ways that you can attract people to you and your nature. You may also attract a certain type of people, but there are efforts you can make to go out and meet people (Kidscape, n.d.):

- You can join a club doing something you really enjoy to meet people that have the same interests that you have.

- When making friends, be to them what you hope for them to be to you. Be kind, listen, and show appreciation.

- Choose your friends wisely. It's important to make sure your friends have the same goals and objectives in life as you do or else you may find yourself with a broken friendship because you went into opposite directions as people.

Keeping Good Friends Close

Finding and having good friends does take work. Once you leave school, you and your existing friends tend to go into different directions. But it is important to know and identify who your close friends are. These are the friends with whom you put in the most effort to stay in touch and who also puts in the effort to stay in touch with you!

Family

Even more important than your friends is your family, even though you may not realize it yet. Far too often we live our lives trying to get away from our family, and it is only when we're older and wiser that we realize the only ones that will always have our back are our families.

Your Safe Harbor

There are going to be moments in life when you may face difficulties, but the one certainty that you have is that your family is your place of safety that will always have your support. If there is ever a time that you feel like you have done something that is so awful that your parents will never forgive you, one certainty that I can give you is that your parents will always be there. Yes, they may be disappointed or upset, but they will always love you. One thing that is important is that you need to be able to turn to someone in your family. Speak to your parents, be open with them, and I guarantee that they will always be there to help out. They will also be glad that you could turn to them instead of away from them when you find yourself in a difficult situation.

It is too easy to fit into the movie teenager life of being annoyed with your parents all the time. But there is one piece of valuable information that I can give to you—make sure you have a relationship with your parents that never ends with regrets. Never find yourself later in life thinking, "I should've spent more time with my parents" or "I should have expressed my love to them more openly." Regrets are hard to live with, so try to never have any.

Dating

Yet another complex part of human existence is dating. And whether you are at the phase in your life where you are considering dating or not, at some point, these thoughts are bound to cross your mind. But the thing about dating is that there is a fine line between dating for companionship, dating for fun, and dating with specific intentions for longer commitment in your mind.

At a young age, the most important thing that I would like to tell you about dating is that *there is no rush.* There is no urgency to date or to find "the one," especially if you have other goals in mind. Focus on where you are, where you are going, and what you hope to achieve before you tether yourself to another person just because everyone else in your life seems to be dating.

With that being said, the time for dating will inevitably come. And when it does, you need to be ready to make the right choices. Whether you are dating for marriage or just dating for companionship or because you really like someone, it will matter—maybe not to the world, but it will to you.

Choosing the Right Person

While there are some obvious signs of whether or not you should be with someone, there are some deeper things you should consider. The obvious things would be not dating someone if you don't like them in an intimate or romantic way. It is never a good thing to lead someone on or date them because you don't know how to let them down. Every relationship you have, whether it is family relationships, friendships, or romantic relationships, all reflect a part of who you are. For that reason, it is important to make these relationships count.

Finding the right person entails (Cjco, 2020)

- Finding a relationship that adds value to your life. You don't want to be embarrassed, frustrated, or tired because of a relationship, and while you want a relationship to fit seamlessly into your life, you want to take joy in "putting in the work."

- Next, before you involve someone else into the intricacies and the unique complexities of your life, you need to know who you are first. This will prevent you from basing your identity on someone else. You are your own person, and anyone else should just add to who you already are.

- You need to know what you want from a relationship, and if this doesn't match up with the person you are hoping to become romantically involved with, chances are, your relationship is not going to bring any benefits to either of you.

- Boundaries are important in any relationship. Set clear boundaries that you do not compromise on.

Going on a Date

If it is your first date or your tenth date, there is some etiquette that you should follow, the most important of which is making sure that you don't make your date feel like you're distracted or uninterested. Stay off your phone and give attention where attention is due.

If it is your first date, be sure to split the bill. This creates a notion of no expectations. Once you are comfortable enough with the person you are on a date with, you can then offer to pay for the entire date or accept their offer to do so. But also never expect that they alone will pay for the date.

Additionally, there are some rules that will help you make sure your date goes well:

1. Always be punctual. Your time and their time is valuable.

2. Be honest about what you want from a relationship, and don't take offense when their goals don't line up with yours.

3. Remember that body language speaks volumes. Don't be afraid to let your body language fill in the blanks. If you don't like the person in a romantic way, keep your distance physically, and if you do like them, make eye contact.

4. Your safety is everything. If anything feels slightly off or you get a bad vibe, make it known to someone (for example, send a text to a friend) and remove yourself from the date immediately.

Breaking Up

As if dating wasn't hard enough already, add to it the fact that it rarely happens when the first person you date is the person you end up with for the rest of your life. There are those lucky few in life who marry their high school sweetheart and live their lives having only dated one person, but if you find yourself not being that person, you will have to face the unfortunate reality of going through a breakup.

The honest truth is that you will rarely go through a breakup without hurting yourself or the other person. So don't try to save an unsalvageable relationship just to avoid hurting the other person.

Be clear, open, and honest about the fact that you are breaking up. You don't want them to think you're on a break and everything falls apart for other reasons that involve miscommunication.

It is important to let the person know the reason why you are breaking up, whether it is because you have outgrown each other or if it's because you don't see yourself with them.

In the same way, you may find yourself on the receiving end of a breakup. It is important to face your feelings in the moment and don't try to take revenge or hurt the other person. Just in the same way you'd want someone to accept your feelings, you need to accept their feelings, too.

Then it is time to start the moving on process. It is never easy, and you don't need to pretend to be brave. Feel whatever it is you need to feel. Go through your emotions. It is good and healthy for you.

Staying Safe

Your safety is of utmost importance, whether it is your physical safety, your emotional safety, keeping your digital space safe, or staying safe within your friends, family, and relationships. Here are some safety tips that could go a long way should the need ever arise:

- Always carry some form of safety gear, such as pepper spray or using your keys for self-defense.

- Try not to place yourself in vulnerable situations, such as walking in an alley alone after dark. Stick with friends and make sure that someone knows where you are at all times.

- If you feel unsafe in any situation, always tell someone or call someone you trust to help remove you from the situation.

- Protect your digital space with passwords that only you remember.

- If you find yourself being victimized in any way, in any of the relationships you may have, it is always important to speak to someone. If you are too afraid to speak to someone you know, there are always people that you can call.

Social Media

Social media is such an important part of life. It is even a platform used for businesses and schools and removing yourself from social media spaces may not always be feasible. In such cases, here are some pointers that you can employ to make sure that you use social media effectively:

- Not every aspect of your life needs to be shared on social media.

- Give yourself a break from social media, even if it is just limiting yourself to a few minutes a day on a social media app.

- Your safety on social media is of utmost importance. If removing certain people is important for your mental health, don't be afraid to do so.

- Social media should not, in any way, control or rule your life.

- Don't share any personal information with anyone on social media, even if you think you know them.

- If you won't be comfortable with the world seeing or knowing something, don't share that on social media, even if it is just with one person.

- Try not to keep secrets from your parents. If something seems strange or suspicious, you may be the last person to realize it. Telling your parents about certain occurrences may set off alarm bells for them and could keep you and your friends safe.

- Don't use social media to hurt others. If you wouldn't like someone doing something to you, be sure not to do that same thing to them.

- If you find yourself yearning for or craving social media, it may be a sign that you need to detach. Remember that social media is not an actual person, and you can live without it.

Going Out

One of the important aspects of socializing is the notion of going out or attending or hosting a social gathering. While this is what may usually come to mind when you think of being sociable, it could just mean sitting at home with a few friends, eating pizza, and watching movies.

However, it is important to know how to throw, host, or plan a soiree or a night on the town.

For example, let's say you are heading out for dinner, to go dancing, or to meet friends for a movie. There are some things you need to consider before you actually head out.

1. First, you need to plan and make arrangements with your friends, partner, or family well in advance so that everyone can make space in their personal calendars. Sometimes this will be tricky, and you may need to plan weeks or months ahead. Making sure everyone is on the same page is the best thing you can do.

2. Take initiative. If you find that you haven't seen or spoken to your friends in a while, it may be time for you to send a message in that group and see how everyone is doing and if they'd be happy to meet up. If you are missing them and haven't seen them in a while, they are probably feeling the same way.

3. Once you set a date and everyone's calendars line up, make the reservation and do whatever else you can to solidify a date. With a plan decided on and set in place well in advance, it will make it less likely for anyone to cancel.

4. If you find your friends reaching out to you, try to avoid making it seem like you're too busy to interact with

them. If they are important enough to you, you can find the time to see them.

5. When you're out with friends, it's important that you don't need to feel like you're forced to talk about or do something. Also, spend within your limit… You don't need to keep up with anyone if it is out of your budget.

If you are planning on hosting a party or an event, things may be slightly different than planning to head out to a neutral place with your friends. If you are hosting an event, remember that you are responsible for making sure that everyone is taken care of and fed. Don't expect people to bring their own food, meals, or drinks unless they offer.

Also, you will need to plan for the event extensively. You will first need to have a guest list in place. Once you have a list, you know how many people to cater for. Tip: an important thing to note if you are inviting people over or if you are invited, always check how many guests will be attending and if you can bring an extra person with. It's just courtesy to do so.

Next, you're going to need to plan the details of the event such as what theme will it be (if there will be a theme at all), what the food and entertainment will be, what do you need for the event (such as cutlery, crockery, food, and drinks), and you will need to set a budget in place.

Lastly, planning an event can be a lot of work. As the host, you may find yourself too busy to actually enjoy the event. To avoid this happening, plan as much as possible in advance so that nothing needs to be done when your guests arrive and so that you can enjoy the company immediately, and you should ask for help or take the help that is offered whenever you may need it. If you have extra help, it may make it easy for your event to happen seamlessly and for you to enjoy as much of it as possible.

And with that, I have hopefully touched on every important aspect of your social life that may exist. However, as I mentioned, one's social life is extremely complex. It would be impossible for me to cover all the nuances and occurrences that you may be currently facing or will face in future.

However, being equipped with the basic skills can help you thrive in almost every social situation and emerge as the social butterfly you know you are. Alternatively, it will also help you respectfully turn down an invite so that you can live your best and most comfortable introverted life.

With that said, another important part of life is your physical health. Let us explore this topic and delve into things that are sometimes avoided because society may get uncomfortable around these topics. Let us talk about everything that may make your life great.

Chapter 3: Physical Health

To keep the body in good health is a duty… otherwise we shall not be able to keep the mind strong and clear. –Buddha

Our physical health is often taken for granted. Perhaps you're at the age where you can eat whatever you want and you don't gain any weight. And while that is great, does it really mean that you are healthy considering the junk you put into your body?

You see, people often have the false notion that you need to be fat, slow, or tire easily to be unhealthy. But, this is not the case.

Maintaining your physical health is a unique combination of eating well, exercising, taking care of your mind, and taking care of your soul. I know this may seem like a lot of work, and you may already be rolling your eyes at the thought of heading to the gym, but hear me out—staying healthy doesn't need to entail spending half your life at the gym and eating cardboard.

The starting point of a healthy lifestyle is realizing that everyone is different. What works for your friend to stay healthy may not work for you, or you may not enjoy what she does to stay healthy and that will mean that you will find it hard to stick to those health regiments.

Perhaps even while you're reading this you're finding it hard to find the motivation you need to get up and get active. But what if I told you that being active and staying healthy don't need to feel like a tiring chore? What if I told you that there aren't huge changes that you need to make to your current lifestyle to get healthier? And what if I told you that once you find your groove and your habits, it gets easier to maintain?

This is not a scam, and no matter what stage of your life you're in right now, whether you're in school, in college, or working, staying healthy can easily integrate into your life.

Eating Healthy

When you think of eating healthy, you may think of dry and flavorless salads that are destined to keep you starving. If this is what comes to mind, your idea of and relationship with food need to change. Remember, you are not starting or going on a diet. Instead, you are aiming toward eating healthier overall.

Eating healthy is actually a commitment that you need to make to your body and your overall health. You need to remember that you're not just doing it now so that you fit into your prom dress or so you look good at spring break. You are implementing a healthy lifestyle so that when you are older, you are able to do the things you were able to do when you were younger.

There are many ways that you can pursue a healthier lifestyle, from eating healthier food, making use of different lifestyle practices, doing exercise on a regular basis, and much more. Here are some healthy habits you could form:

- Eat more fruits and vegetables. This may seem like an obvious one, but they are packed with nutrients, fiber, and everything else that your body needs to thrive. You can also eat fruit and some vegetables on the go, which means less time in the kitchen if cooking isn't something you particularly enjoy.

- Try to have more balanced meals. I don't mean having a candy bar in one hand and a bag of chips in the other hand because that isn't a balanced meal. Instead, try to have meals that are made up of vegetables, proteins, a healthy carb, and healthy fats. The more meals that you eat that are balanced, the healthier you will find your body being.

- Reduce your sugar. Who doesn't love sugar? Unfortunately, it doesn't do well for your body. Cutting down your overall intake of sugar will do a world of good for your health.

- Probably the most important health tip you will ever hear is drink enough water. This cannot be emphasized enough. It is needed for you to function and for you to be effective in your daily task. I could tell you how your body is made up of more than 60% water (Water Science School, 2019), or you can realize that drinking water must be important, especially since people tell you to drink it so much.

- Do not miss breakfast. I know how easy it is to run late in the mornings, and while you can't skip a shower or brush your hair, the one thing you can skip is breakfast. But this isn't true. Skipping breakfast can throw your entire blood sugar balance out of whack, and it can leave you feeling horrible and tired. Eating a healthy breakfast will prove extremely beneficial to your energy levels and your mental acuity throughout the day.

- While takeout is convenient and food that you haven't made tastes so good, try to limit your takeout consumption to once or twice a month. When you cook food, it is easy to see exactly what is going into your meal.

- Eat healthy snacks between meals and you may find yourself craving less junk food.

- Planning your meals for each day, as tedious as it sounds, actually results in there being no guesswork or you resorting to getting takeout because you didn't plan.

- Keep your meals high in protein. Protein keeps your muscles fed, helps you burn fat, and keeps you fuller for longer.

- Eat slower. It gives your body and your metabolism time to keep up with all the food that is coming into your mouth.

- Try something new. When you are trying to stay healthy, it is easy to get tired and frustrated with the food you are eating. Try to cook one new recipe every other week to add some excitement to the task of cooking.

You Are What You Eat

There is a well-known adage that says "you are what you eat." This doesn't mean that you are french fries or burgers, but what it does mean is what you put into your body is ultimately what you are going to get out. There are foods that you will eat that make you slow down and feel more tired, and there are foods that will make you feel good, lighter, and healthier.

But this saying is quite direct and easy to understand. It means that if you want to live a good and healthy life you need to eat healthy foods and put things of sustenance into your body.

If you don't believe me, do a comparison for yourself. Compare how you feel after a good and healthy meal with how you feel after eating junk food. My recommendation to you would be to continue eating what makes you feel good.

Sleep

Aside from eating well and doing exercise, something that is vital for your survival is sleep. It is no coincidence that as humans, we are designed to spend one-third of our lives sleeping. This is because important things happen when your body rests.

Why Is Sleep Important?

Something you may not have realized or you may not have given much attention to is the fact that your body and bodily functions never ever stop. When does your heart stop beating? Never! When do your lungs stop taking in air? Never! In fact, the only time these things happen in your body are when you are no longer alive. But for as long as you are alive, this never stops. The same is true for your brain.

Your brain never stops functioning, not even when you're sleeping. But sleeping is important because it gives your brain the opportunity to power down some functions that are actively working and take a break. For example, your brain controls everything, even your breathing and your heartbeat. But these functions are almost like automated systems in your body. When you're awake, your brain controls other functions in addition to these automated systems, such as seeing and processing sight from your eyes, problem-solving, and formulating thoughts that you will either use in your day job or that you will need to communicate to others, and so much more.

Now while your brain doesn't stop working when you're asleep, it does power down all unnecessary functions like sensory input and literally goes into sleep mode. When it is in sleep mode, your brain starts healing itself, resting, filtering out all toxins and heightened functions that it experienced during the day, and optimizing itself for the next day.

Your brain also begins resetting all functions. In the day, your body produces and uses a variety of hormones, your metabolism runs at different paces, and your body goes through stresses at various points of the day (National Heart, Lung, and Blood Institute, 2022). During sleep, it resets all functions back to zero so that you can start each new day on a clean slate.

Quality Over Quantity

You may have heard that you need to get more sleep. A general rule of thumb is that you should get around eight hours of sleep. Maybe you have slept for a really long time but then woke up in the morning feeling strangely tired? This is probably because you had a lot of sleep but not good quality sleep. So while it is great to get eight hours of sleep every night, it's not much use if your quality of sleep is poor (Kohyama, 2021).

What is good quality sleep? Well, unlike measuring the hours you have slept, sleep quality is a scientific measurement that accounts for multiple factors (Suni, 2020). This includes factors such as

- How restful was your sleep?

- How restful do you feel after waking up?

- Do you crave more sleep?

- Did you have a deep sleep?

- Are you able to sleep for the duration of time you're supposed to spend sleeping?

- Do you wake up only once or more than once at night?

- Are you able to sleep immediately after waking in the middle of the night?

While these are just some of the tools used to measure sleep quality, more detailed studies can be done on you at a sleep clinic, but these are just ways for you to measure if you are getting quality sleep.

How to Get Good Quality Sleep?

So, now that you know what good quality sleep is, how do you get it? It's not like clothes where, now that you know what the difference between good quality and bad quality is, you can just head out to the store and pick up some good quality sleep. No, unfortunately with sleep, it's a bit trickier because you need to know what to change and adjust so that you do get good quality sleep.

Here are some tips that you can implement in your lifestyle that may drastically increase the quality of sleep you get (CDC, 2016):

- Try to get into a consistent routine. We have already spoken about routines in previous chapters, and that will be further emphasized here. Be sure to have consistent sleep and wake times, whether it is school or work days, weekends, or vacations. I know, by the time the weekend rolls around, you want to binge-watch series late into the night and wake up late the next morning. What ultimately ends up happening is that your entire sleep routine is thrown off.

- The environment in which you sleep needs to be optimal. You see, your mind associates bright lights with daytime and awake time, and it associates dark spaces with sleeping time. In fact, your body actually begins releasing specific hormones toward the evening time as it gets darker that works with your circadian rhythm, which actually links your sleeping with the light levels outside. This means that you should set the mood for sleep time in your room. Keep the room dark, have very few items in it to keep you relaxed and to prevent you from becoming overstimulated, and make sure the room is at a comfortable temperature. In general, a space that is too cold or too hot will make it difficult to sleep. Optimize the temperature in your room, and you will have great sleep.

- While you may feel sleepy after eating a big, fat, greasy meal and may think that you're going to have a great sleep after that meal, this is not always the case. It is best to avoid large and heavy meals, and especially caffeinated drinks before bedtime. Eating will trigger your body's digestive system, which is one of the functions that goes into sleep mode when you do sleep. This means that your digestive system will be fighting for resources and energy when it should be relaxing and calming down. Depending on what wins this battle, you may have a restless sleep because your body is actively digesting food, or you may find yourself gaining weight because your brain shut down your digestive system so it could rest.

- Everyone feels a nice sense of calm and tiredness after engaging in rigorous exercise. One of the best ways to help you get a deeper sleep is to engage in exercise during the day. It will make your body tired enough to fall into a deep sleep.

Exercise

Some people love it, some people hate it, but everyone needs it—exercise. It is an extremely important part of living a healthy life. Our bodies weren't meant to sit still for eight hours and do absolutely nothing. Before technology, office jobs, and everything else we have now, humans were hunters and gatherers. This means that we were designed to survive by using our bodies and movement because the only way we would survive was to physically gather and hunt for our food.

Now, while this has changed, it is through no fault of our own but rather the ever-adapting and ever-evolving climate of society. Survival and success are no longer measured by what they were in the past, and the only way to put a value to this success is by the financial and monetary gains you make. How do you get those monetary gains? By working in an office or having a business. This means that we spend more time sitting still than we do moving.

But there are ways to make up for this. Engaging in physical activity is extremely important. Whether you sign up at the gym or for an extracurricular activity, getting some form of physical movement is important for your health.

Benefits of Exercise

All of the previously mentioned points work together in tandem to create a healthier body for you. So you will see many of the benefits of exercise mirrored here as you have seen it in previous sections of this chapter.

These are some of the benefits that exercise provides you with:

- It keeps your brain functioning at maximum acuity. This is because it releases feel-good hormones, minimizes stress hormones, and increases the oxygen supply to your brain.

- If your goal is to get summer ready and work on your spring break or vacation body, then exercise is one of the best ways to do this. By exercising, you can lose weight and keep the weight off.

- It minimizes heart disease and diabetes.

- It strengthens every part of your body, not just muscles, but bones too!

- Because it releases endorphins, it leads to you just feeling like you're in a better mood.

- Guess what else it does? It improves your quality of sleep (although you already knew that).

You probably know some of these benefits of exercising, yet, often, people still don't get around to it. Some people come up with elaborate excuses for why they can't exercise, and frequently their excuses can be remedied by exercise. Most times people would avoid exercising because

- They are too tired.

- They can't find the time.

- They think they are already healthy or thin so they don't need to exercise.

- They think gym fees cost too much.

- They think they have good genes that will keep them healthy.

First, if you're too tired, you will find exercising gives you more energy. Next, if you can make time to scroll on social media or do the tasks that don't add to or take away from your life, then you can probably make the time to exercise. I am not saying to avoid Instagram completely so you can exercise instead, but a great remedy to this problem would be to take five minutes away from social media and five minutes away from watching TV, and you have ten minutes of exercise time.

Many people think that because they aren't overweight or because they are already healthy, they don't need exercise. But exercise adds years to your life and gives you other benefits that go far beyond health and weight loss.

Lastly, you don't need to go to the gym or spend any money to get exercise. You could take your dog for a walk around your neighborhood, and that is easily considered a workout. You could join your school's gymnastic or cheerleading squad, or you could even do little things like parking further away from the mall entrance. Exercising doesn't need to be expensive and it doesn't need to be a bore.

Hygiene

Something that is extremely important and that is often not talked about because people are too shy or embarrassed is hygiene. Many people don't like talking openly about intimate wear and how one should take care of their body because it may seem too awkward to talk about out loud. Well, luckily for you, you're reading about it in the book which takes the awkwardness away.

Hygiene is all about the important daily practices you employ to maintain your overall health. Most often it is referred to as physical cleanliness. Let me give you an analogy. Let's say you are cooking in your kitchen and some food splashes on the counter. Because you don't pay any mind to any hygiene practices, you don't clean the counter. It stays there for a few days, and when you cook again, more food spills onto the counter. This happens over and over again, and eventually it attracts critters that carry germs. Because this is the place where you cook, you eat from these surfaces and this leads to you getting sick.

While this is probably too disgusting to think of, it is a reality. But it isn't only limited to food hygiene and hygiene in the kitchen. Personal hygiene is extremely important.

There are certain things that you need to do on a daily basis to keep yourself clean and maintain your personal hygiene. This includes having a shower or a bath every day, brushing your teeth, and cleaning your face. This minimizes body odor that may accumulate throughout the day, but these odors, which are perfectly normal, can be further masked by sprays and antiperspirant products.

General Hygiene

There are important things that you need to do every day, perhaps many times a day, to maintain your personal hygiene.

You need to wash your hands often, keep your nails clean, and avoid coughing and sneezing without covering your mouth.

When you shower or bathe, you want to be thorough in cleaning every part of your body, making sure not to forget to clean your ears.

Although your hair doesn't need to be washed on a daily basis, you need to make sure that you wash it often and thoroughly as oils and products build up causing dandruff and other scalp irritations.

Menstrual Hygiene

One of the certainties of life is the fact that every woman, at a certain age, will begin her menstrual cycle and will have a period. Taking proper care of yourself and your body during this time is of paramount importance because your body is not only losing blood, but blood has an odor. Also, if you consider where you menstruation occurs, it is in a dark and humid area of the body that doesn't experience much sunlight, meaning it is the ideal place for bacteria to thrive. This can be avoided by making use of the proper, effective hygiene practices.

The first thing you want to do is keep your genital area clean. Showering or bathing with warm water is usually sufficient as your vagina is a self-cleaning organ. Harsh soaps should be avoided to prevent irritation. Also make use of other hygiene tips such as wiping from front to back whenever you use the bathroom.

Clean your hands before handling any menstrual products or anything else that may come into contact with your genital area. You also want to make sure that when you are experiencing your period cycle, always change your pad or tampons every few hours. This should be done whether you have a heavy or light period flow (CDC, 2022c).

You also want to make sure that when you are in your menstrual period, you wear clothes that don't make you too hot and sweaty because you want to keep your genital area as dry as possible.

Clothes for Hygiene

To maintain your personal hygiene, it is important that you wash your clothes frequently and that you change your clothes every day. This will prevent odors from setting in and making you feel uncomfortable for any reason.

The best way to keep your clothes clean is by washing the clothes that are closest to your skin more often. This means that underwear should be changed daily as should most undergarments or clothes that actually touch your body. Sweaters and jackets can be washed less frequently.

There are some clothes that are good for personal hygiene and others that are not so good. A great rule of thumb is to wear clothes and underwear that are made of cotton because it is a light and breathable fabric. Latex, lace, and extremely elastic materials are not great for hygiene and can often cause skin irritations.

Skin Care

Whether you have an extremely rigorous skin care routine or your skin handles soap and water just fine, it is important to take care of your skin. Drinking enough water, eating healthy, and cleansing your face appropriately will keep your skin in good condition. It is also important never to forget to use sunscreen. It will protect your body from cancer risks and exposure to the elements that you are bound to experience going about your day.

Now that you know how to take care of your space and your physical body, you are on your way to becoming an independent adult. But part of taking care of yourself and your space also means taking care of your mind and your mental health. After all, it may seem like you're drowning under the to-do list of making sure you are healthy and your space is organized. There are ways to deal with and cope with the feelings of overwhelm and stress.

In the next chapter, we are going to look at how you can take care of your mental health.

Chapter 4: Mental Health

"Positive vibes only" isn't a thing. Humans have a wide range of emotions and that's OK. –Molly Bahr, LMHC

In the midst of busy lives and constantly staying active and fulfilling our roles in the lives of those around us, we often forget to take care our mental health.

Sometimes, it's easy to neglect our mind and our emotions because they aren't actually seen or tangible, so we get preoccupied with the things we can see and forget about what we can't.

But for us to stay healthy on the whole, we need to take care of every part of our lives. There is no point in being physically healthy but mentally unhealthy because eventually your mind will affect your body, too.

So what is mental health and why is it important? According to the Center for Disease Control and Prevention (2018), mental health refers to an individual's emotional, psychological, and social health. It is an intangible aspect of your life that is usually impacted by your interactions with others and your ability to handle different forms of stress.

The CDC (2018) also makes a clear distinction between poor mental health and mental illness. While your mental health may be poor because of stress that is temporary, such as studying for an exam or dealing with a misunderstanding among friends and peers, mental illness is usually diagnosed by a medical practitioner and is seen as a chronic problem.

Mental health is also always changing. Some days you may feel down and depressed, but that doesn't mean that you suffer from chronic depression. Just in the same way that our body fights off some ailments like a cold or a flu, our mind also goes through stages where it doesn't feel great. This coupled with the fact that sometimes you may face the loss of a loved one or you go through a breakup often means that your mental health can change, but provided you give it consistent care, much like your body, it can stay healthier for longer.

Focusing on your mental health is important for ensuring that you stay well physically because being burnt out and overworked can eventually start having a negative impact on your health. With all components of life and the body so closely interlinked, it is important to know that one aspect of life is likely to affect the other.

Generally speaking, you want to keep your mental health high and well. Mental health is your mental state at any even given time. You can nurture your mental health and stay in consistently good spirits by engaging in self-care, allowing yourself to rest when you need it, and trying to be an overall positive person. Sometimes circumstances don't allow us to be in excessively good spirits, and that's alright. It's part of the natural ebb and flow of life. In these low moments, your mental health won't be at optimal level, but you still have the power and the potential to nurture your mental health back to its former glory.

Stress and Anxiety

Whether you are in school, college, or working, you have probably felt stress and anxiety in some form. Maybe you feel it in its most severe forms or maybe it is manageable, either way, we experience it. But stress and anxiety are emotions that we are born with. They just ignite feelings that make us uncomfortable or that we'd rather not feel. But anxiety and stress, in healthy doses, are important for our survival.

Both stress and anxiety are important when we are facing situations that need urgent attention or when we are facing situations that our minds perceive as threats. For example, an impending test or examination, a deadline for a project, or an interview. It raises the stakes just enough for us to find the motivation to do our best at that project. In the same way, if you really care about something, chances are, you are going to feel just enough stress and anxiety to push you to do your best.

Sometimes, our experiences of stress and anxiety may not ease up, even after the cause of these feelings has long passed. In those cases, you can pursue activities or different methods of reducing your stress and anxiety. One such method is meditation.

Meditation

Sometimes, our mind just moves a bit too far out of our grasp, and we need to bring it back to a neutral calm space. Being stressed out and having a lot of anxiety can affect your sleep, your health, and your mental headspace. It can affect how you function on a day-to-day basis. Using meditation techniques is a great way of bringing your mind and your stress levels back down. It helps you get a grasp on your mind before you spiral out of control—metaphorically, that is.

Meditation is a tool that is used to ease and calm your mind. It can be used to calm down excessive stress or even excitement. It helps bring you back to a calm space. There are many forms of "formal" meditation practice where you can be instructed on how to breathe and specific mechanisms that have been used in traditional meditation forms.

However, beyond the notion of "formal" or strict meditation practices, meditation can be whatever makes you feel calm and relaxed, whether it is

- listening to calm music and focusing on your breathing

- going on a walk in nature

- doing some yoga

- painting

- doing your favorite hobby

Meditation has the potential to be extremely personal, and you should use the methods that are best for you.

Depression

While your mental health is something that you need to take care of on a daily basis and that moves with you through each stage of life, being elevated on some days and maybe lower or neutral on other days, there are certain aspects related to mental health that may cause long-term and more persistent problems, such as depression.

Depression comes like a looming cloud, without warning. It happens gradually over time so you don't even realize you're in darkness until the cloud bursts and you find yourself drenched in the rain of depression.

As human beings, we are emotionally complex and that is why we go through a myriad of emotions, either feeling happy or sad, or at some complex point in the middle. You also learn as you get older that emotions aren't black and white and you can feel many things at once. The difference between feeling sad and being depressed is that depression becomes a chronic feeling of misery and you find yourself feeling sad even without reason (Goldman, 2019).

It is a lingering and consistent feeling that you just can't shake off. In many cases, it is triggered by a major unexpected change. There are some ways that you can identify depression in yourself and in others (Goldman, 2019):

1. People who are depressed tend to struggle to find enjoyment in the things they usually enjoy. If you find yourself or someone else unable to find joy in the things they once loved, this may be a cause for concern.

2. If you notice a sudden change in eating habits, sleeping habits, and overall energy, this may also be a reason to talk to a doctor.

3. A change in mood and overall demeanor is something to look out for as well as difficulties in making decisions.

4. And last but not least is a symptom you should hope never to encounter in yourself or others, and that is thoughts of suicide. Ideally, you would seek help before reaching the depths of these diseases.

While there is no cure for this condition, you can improve your situation greatly. You would need to work with professionals to find an adequate treatment plan that may involve a combination of medication and psychological treatment.

If you find that you or someone you care about may be facing depression, it is important to reach out to them, let them know that you support them, and then speak to someone you trust or a professional. The sooner you seek help, the better it will be in preventing the depression and its symptoms from spiraling out of control.

Peer Pressure

I'm sure you have heard all about peer pressure. This is emphasized in school and in college and refers to the influences, direct or indirect, positive or negative, that some friends may have on other friends in the same social group. Peer pressure can happen in the form of one person influencing others or more than one person, and it is most commonly referred to in the negative context.

Perhaps as you're reading this, you're thinking that you're probably past the age at which you can be influenced and that you know better. But believe it or not, even adults can succumb to peer pressure.

The solution to overcoming peer pressure is to be comfortable in your own skin, know who you are, and don't try to change, bend, or buckle under the weight of someone else's opinion. But why is this the solution? You see, when experiencing peer pressure, your views on the world are ultimately altered. It could be your beliefs or even how you act and the things you do.

Succumbing to peer pressure can have major implications because on a deeper level, it can make you go against the very thing that makes you you. It can influence your future by impacting the choices and decisions you make and can even end in the most catastrophic ways. It can change the way you interact with other people, and when you look back in time after years have passed, you may find yourself ashamed of your behavior.

Sometimes, it is impossible to avoid peer pressure. Maybe the person who is putting this pressure on you is one of your best friends, they're in your class, or you see them every day. This can make it nearly impossible to avoid it. So, in cases where you can't avoid it, you need to assert yourself. Here are some ways to help you overcome peer pressure (Lyness, 2018):

- Have your own sense of agency to know and stick to what is right. Knowing and understanding when behavior is inappropriate is a great way to stop yourself from actually being pressured into doing something.

- It's easier to stand up to others when you have someone on your side. If you and your friends can see and identify negative peer pressure, stand up to others.

- Peer pressure can be entirely avoided if you surround yourself with people who are like-minded and have the same values as you do. This may be hard to sift out, but it is easier to choose a few good friends than stick with bad company for popularity.

- Speak to someone or get help when you feel like the situation is getting out of hand. It is easy to say that school is meant for learning and you shouldn't worry about friends and what their opinions are, but the reality is that school, college, and even work are very social environments. Making friends is important, interacting with others is important, and integrating with different people is important. But never be afraid to raise your concerns with someone you can trust, especially if it involves behavior with which you are not comfortable.

Self-Esteem

Directly related to all these points is how you feel about yourself. Depression, stress, anxiety, and peer pressure can all influence the way you feel about yourself. It can impact the relationship you have with yourself, but conversely, if you are in good spirits, have positive mental health, and avoid or overcome peer pressure, it can make you feel good about yourself.

The way you feel about yourself is generally referred to as your self-esteem. It can impact your confidence in your abilities, being certain in yourself and who you are. There are things that will impact your self-esteem, including your physical appearance, your outcome on certain tasks like getting an A on an exam, or completing a task before a deadline.

Your self-esteem can vary from day to day, but generally, it is best to have your self-esteem be directed internally rather than externally. What this means is the best way for you to maintain high levels of confidence is to not base your value, your worth, or your thoughts of yourself on the opinions of others. I know this is hard to do because, often, when someone tells us something, it is so easy to believe them, but your self-esteem is measured against your own view of yourself.

The best way to recognize your self-worth and maintain a high self-esteem is to do a few things at the end of each day:

1. Think about the day and what has caused you to feel good or bad about yourself. This can be related to your physical appearance, your mental abilities, or your social interactions.

2. Acknowledge that you may have faced some instances in the day when people said positive or negative things about you and remind yourself that what other people think about you is not your problem.

3. At the end of the day, tally up all the things that you did on that day that you are proud of. If you managed to top your last grade in math, add that to this list. Even if you managed to do your hair particularly well that morning, add it to the list of wins, too. Find things—little or big—to be proud of and it will become easier and easier.

4. Go out of your way to be kind to yourself. We always make an effort to be kind to others, but if you said to others what you say to yourself, would they think you were a kind person? Before you say anything critical toward yourself, step back and consider the situation if you said those words to someone else.

5. Lastly, one of the best ways to build up your self-esteem is to surround yourself with positive people. If you find yourself feeling awkward or not liking certain things

about yourself after spending time with a specific friend, then maybe you need to reconsider their role in your life.

Addiction

There is a scourge in our world. No matter what age you are, you probably know someone or know of someone who is battling with addiction. Addiction comes in many different forms whether it is an addiction to drugs or alcohol, and it usually is one of the hardest things in the world to overcome.

There are some things you can keep an eye out for if you suspect a friend or someone you know may be battling addiction. First, you'd want to keep an eye out for any out of the ordinary behavioral and personality changes. They may portray many differences in their personality, such as lashing out at you, acting like they are not occupying the same space as you, or becoming strangely calm or aggressive. They may also seem agitated and even anxious about things in everyday life. This is why observations of those around you are so important. Make a point of actually wanting to know how your friends are doing.

If you aren't sure if someone is addicted because they may be hiding their behavior, you can use other information to help you. To identify addiction or even approach this with someone, you need to know what their normal personality is. This is because addiction can send them into any direction either way from what they are usually like. For example, if you know someone to be generally pleasant, addiction could cause them to become aggressive or even extra happy, which is usually what makes identifying addiction really difficult to do.

Another challenge that comes with those fighting addiction is that, as a friend, all you can do is support them and let them know that you are there to help them overcome their addiction and challenges. If someone finds themselves in a situation where they are addicted to substances, they may not even realize the extent of their addiction until they are in too deep. Addiction affects so many aspects of life. It impacts your ability to function, it severs relationships, and it changes people. But seeking help to overcome addiction can only come from the person themselves. It usually takes something bad happening for them to realize the severity of their addiction. All you can do is make an active effort to support the person you care about. Let them know that you see the change and alteration it is making to who they are as a person, and let them know that you will help them overcome this addiction no matter what it takes!

They may not turn to you immediately, but you may be the person that helps them later on.

In the midst of learning all about life, sometimes you have to learn things that aren't pleasant, like encountering addiction or depression. But knowing about this is a way of making sure you are equipped with dealing with these challenges if you do ever face them.

If you find yourself needing help, you can call the National Suicide Prevention Lifeline: 1-800-273-8255. If you need support in helping a friend with addiction, you can call the Substance Abuse and Mental Health Services Administration (SAMHSA): 1-800-662-4257. Also, reach out to local resources or counselors at your school or workplace for assistance.

Chapter 5: Financial Skills

Money is a terrible master but an excellent servant. –P.T. Barnum

The world revolves around money. This isn't a bad thing—it just means that to buy things in the world, you need to earn money. Because of its importance, we should know how to handle and take care of our money. The only problem is they don't teach us the things we need to know at school. In this chapter, we are going to delve into the intricacies of finances, and you will learn some tips that will help you make smart financial decisions.

Employment vs. Entrepreneurship

The world is constantly developing, but one thing that remains certain is that you need money to buy things. To get money, you need to work. There are rarely any instances where people have had large amounts of money fall into their laps.

There are many ways to earn money. Some people may follow traditional career paths, while others may follow different, creative approaches to earning money.

The two most common paths that people follow are either employment, where you apply and use your skills while working at an organization, or using your skills to establish your own business. Each of these career paths come with their own unique challenges and benefits, and ultimately, the path you choose will depend on the person you are and the goals you hope to fulfill.

Employment

If you decide to obtain employment from an organization, essentially you would be working for someone else in the company they have established. It may not be a privately owned organization. You could be employed at a government organization, educational institute, or anywhere else where you are not the owner.

Some of the benefits of being employed by someone else are that you have a set and steady income and working hours. This means that every week or month, you can expect a paycheck of a set amount, and you have a regular start and end time each day. When your work day ends, you can shut off your "work" mind and do personal tasks that are completely unrelated to work.

In addition to getting paid, you also get other benefits, such as health insurance, the possibility for upward growth within the company, and skills to enhance your career, particularly in the context of the company in which you're working. Companies often have programs to fund education opportunities or specialized training or certifications relevant to your field..

The organization at which you work will also take care of many administrative functions, such as making sure your tax is sorted out and that the appropriate deductions have been made.

While there is some job security that comes with employment, there is still the risk of downsizing or losing your job. However, in many cases, if you are working at an organization that has been well established for a long time, that is a government entity, or that has processes set in place to minimize downsizing, you don't need to be too worried about losing your job.

Additionally, other challenges that you may face are that you have no control over your work environment or over the organization at all. Also, you have to deal with colleagues and the challenges you may face with them, such as disagreements. You may even find your creativity and your own initiative somewhat pushed down and limited in the context of the organization at which you are working.

Entrepreneurship

It would be great to imagine showing up to work after lunch and leaving an hour later, telling people what to do, and reaping the financial rewards because you're the owner of the organization. But this is a very false idea of what it takes to be an entrepreneur.

An entrepreneur is someone who establishes their own company. They find a need and they fulfill that need. One of the best things about being an entrepreneur is that you get to control all of your organization's finances and operations. While you can hire experts to oversee specific functions within your organization, you still get the final say in the decisions pertaining to your organization.

As an entrepreneur, you develop multiple skills that are required to keep your company running. For example, if you own a business that sells candles, you will not only have expertise in candle making, but you will also develop skills related to finance so that you manage the flow of cash in your business. You also get a lot more schedule and financial flexibility. If you choose to have your company start its work day at 10 a.m. and close at 6 p.m., provided all the work gets done, you can do so.

However, there is a lot of financial strain that comes with being an entrepreneur. To establish your own company, you need to have enough capital to cover start-up costs and then you need to make sure that you make enough profit to keep your business running. You also may not make any money for yourself because you need to make sure that your employees are taken care of first.

It takes a lot of hard work to build your own business compared to starting a job as an employee at an organization.

Something that is also great to remember is that being an entrepreneur doesn't have to follow the traditional concepts of selling products and having a factory or whatever thoughts may come to mind when you think of an entrepreneur. Instead, you can be one person that owns a business and works as a freelancer or as an artist and a creative, selling the artwork that you make.

Paying Bills

One of the most adult things you could do is pay your bills. It is both a privilege and an annoyance, but it certainly puts your name on the map as someone who exists in this world and who is a functioning member of society.

There are a few things that you should know about paying bills:

- Bills are payments for things that you need. Before you incur any debts or bills, you first need to make sure they are necessary and that you can afford them.

- The best way to assess if you can afford to pay your bills is to make a monthly or weekly budget, depending on how often you get paid. You are then going to record all money that comes into your bank account and weigh up your expenses against your income.

- Paying your bills doesn't have to feel like a tedious task, and in most cases, you can set up automated payments on your cell phone. All you need to do is arrange with your bank that payment for fixed amount bills are sent on a specific date, and it is always recommended that the payment of your bills take place as soon after your income reflects in your account. This makes sure that priority payments are made and whatever money you have left over can be used for savings and spending.

How to Budget

Budgeting is extremely important for staying financially healthy and for maintaining your financial independence. As much as your parents would do anything to support you, it is always good to try to be as financially self-sufficient as possible.

One way of ensuring this financial health is by budgeting. Budgeting is basically a way of keeping track of your income and expenses and making sure that all money has an allocated purpose. This means that even if you are expecting to have money left over, you should probably allocate it to spending or to savings so that it has a purpose.

Budgeting is a task that is done so that you know where your money is going and so that you can account for your money going to different places. Preparing a budget is quite simple, but it does require you to pay close attention to every single movement of your finances. Here is how you can begin creating your budget (Bank of America, 2019):

1. The first thing you're going to do is track your income. If you are employed, chances are, you will receive the same income every month or every week, which will be your salary or your wages. However, if you are an entrepreneur, you may have an income that varies. In this case, keep track for several weeks or months to find the average weekly or monthly income to use for budgeting.

2. Once you know what your income is, you are going to minus compulsory deductions that may be automatically taken off from your salary, such as tax, health insurance, or any other amounts that get taken off from your salary. Once you subtract these deductions, you will be left with what is known as your net income.

3. Now you are going to begin tracking your spending. Budgets are living documents that change and adapt almost constantly. The only way for you to get an accurate estimation on how much you spend on average for different expenses is to track your spending over a few months and calculate the average. Either way, you are going to make a detailed note of expenses and bills that need to be paid, whether they are running expenses or once-off expenses.

4. Next, you're going to establish goals on how your money will be allocated. You want to account for all your needed expenses, for savings, and for spending (which includes heading out for dinner with friends, buying a birthday gift, or going shopping).

5. Then you're going to plan how you're going to execute your budgetary plan. If it means that you have to sacrifice one night out with your friends for the month to meet your financial goals, then you need to consider doing so. Having a plan in place will allow you to realize when you need to say no to spending certain things and when you don't need to say no.

6. Because your budget will differ month-to-month because of expenses (such as sending your car for a service, buying your mom a birthday gift, or going to the

hairdresser), it is important for you to constantly review your budget and update it whenever you need to. If you find that you are struggling to survive if you're saving a certain percentage of your income, perhaps you need to reconsider adjusting your budget to reduce your monthly savings or assess where you can cut down on certain expenses.

Loans and Investments

On the path to financial stability, you may encounter the concept of investments and loans. Investments are the idea of putting money either into an account or into a company with the hopes that it grows and earns interest so that when you cash out your investment, it is a bigger amount than you initially put in.

Investments

Investments are a great way to grow your money in a passive way. There are many investment options that you can pursue. If you are younger, you may not have accumulated enough money to invest into anything big such as property or opening up an extensive investment portfolio consisting of stocks and bonds. Instead, when you start getting money, whether it is getting an allowance from your parents or a weekend job that you are working, try saving up to 20% of that money, no matter how much or how little you are getting.

Next, you are going to open a savings account with the money you have accumulated. Once you open the savings account, you will start earning interest on the money you have and this will be your first actual investment. Granted, it will be small, but one thing that is guaranteed to secure your financial growth and investments later on is if you start saving early in life.

Think about it this way: You and your friend are both 25 years old. You started saving $5 a month from the time you turned 13, but your friend only started saving $5 a month from the age of 16. You would have saved $720 by the time you reach the age of 25 and your friend would have only saved $540. You are both the same age, saving the exact same amount of money, but you started earlier. Don't get me wrong, it's never too late to start, but starting now is better than starting in three months' time.

Once you have started earning interest on your savings account, you may find that you are in a position to expand your investment portfolio. Maybe you are earning more money because you have gotten a steady job. Now you can find companies to invest in, you can invest in stocks and yield dividends from these shares, you can begin purchasing properties, and you can even move your funds into high-yield savings or investments accounts.

Nonfinancial Investments

While you can make a number of monetary or financial investments, you can even invest in some assets that grow in value over time. Financial or monetary investments are also things such as retirement savings accounts. These investments are known as intangible investments. But when you invest in assets that appreciate in value over time, these are referred to as tangible assets. I know the first thought that may come to mind is buying a car, but a car loses a lot of value over time. Instead, you want to invest in items that appreciate in value. These are items such as art, collectible items, and even luxury or couture items of jewelry.

One investment that often goes by unnoticed and that is often forgotten about is an investment that never loses its value and that gradually appreciates in value. That investment is *you*.

Investing in yourself can come in many ways. It can look like self-care or paying a substantial amount to get your hair done before a job interview. However, while these physical investments are great and often well-deserved, they do depreciate in value because your nails may chip or your highlights may fade and grow out. But you can invest in yourself in a way that doesn't lose value by taking courses to upskill, enrolling in different forms of training exercises, and picking up new abilities, working hard to perfect those abilities, and using those abilities to earn a return on the investment you made into yourself.

There is only one you in this world. You are the only person who has all the skills and abilities you have. No one can do what you do the way you can do it. Use these unique abilities to increase your prospects for future gain.

Once you learn a piece of knowledge or a skill, it stays with you forever. If you take courses and gain certification in certain skills, you will have that education with you forever.

Loans

On the opposite end of the financial spectrum are loans. Loans are when you borrow money from a lender or a financial institute, and you are expected to pay the amount back in full and with interest. When you take out a loan, it is usually considered a debt and is something that should be added to your list of expenses when you are establishing your budget.

There are multiple different loans that you could take that serve a number of purposes and that often have a wide range of interest rates attached to them:

- a student loan, which can be used to pay for your studies

- a small personal loan

- a bigger loan, such as a mortgage to pay for your home

- a credit card, which is also considered to be a loan

Credit Cards

We all know what credit cards are. They are these magic little things that have unlimited amounts of funds that we can use to buy clothes and shoes and everything else that is great, right? This couldn't be further from the truth. A credit card provides access to money, but it is not unlimited, and like a loan, it has to be paid back—with interest.

Also, in the same way that different forms of loans exist, there are various types of credit cards. If your parents have a credit card, you are unable to use it unless you are an authorized user. You see, having the pin to use the card is not enough. If you have not been authorized to use the credit card, it can be flagged as fraud and that is a serious crime to commit.

Every month, your credit card statement will give you a minimum amount that is required to be paid. It is important to make the minimum payment, or more if you can afford it, so that you don't incur major interest charges.

The reason why use of a credit card is so restricted is because, even over and above the money that has been "borrowed," your credit card can actually be used as a way to store your extra money, by putting some funds in your credit card account.

Credit Score

A credit card sounds great, but how do you get one? Unfortunately, they aren't just giving them out. And maybe that's not a bad thing. You see, to qualify for a credit card, you need to have an established credit rating. What a credit rating does is tell potential lenders what kind of borrower you are. It tells them whether you are trustworthy, if you pay your bills on time, and if you pay more or less than the amount that is due.

It isn't easy to build up a worthy reputation or credit score, especially because in order to take most of your first loans, you need a credit score history, but to get credit score, you need to have a credit card or be paying off some form of credit. This presents you with a bit of a catch-22 situation.

But there are solutions to this problem. You could apply for a starter credit card or a student credit card that you can be enrolled at an academic institute to qualify for, which are there to help you establish and positively affect your credit score while learning how to use credit responsibly (Rathner, 2020).

Checking and Savings Accounts

Today few money transactions happen with actual physical cash. Instead, it all takes place in a digital sphere where we have money in an account and we swipe our cards or tap our phones to pay for items. These transactions will either withdraw from a checking or a savings account.

There is one major difference between a checking and a savings account. A checking account is designed specifically to make transactions whether it is on a daily basis or not. It is the best account from which you can make in-store purchases, is ideal for money transfers, and is great for automated payments.

A savings account, on the other hand, is ideal to do just that—save. If you are storing money or trying to build up your cash stash for an investment as mentioned earlier in this chapter, then a savings account is a great way to save money as you can earn some interest.

Buying a House

So the moment has finally arrived. You are equipped enough to leave the nest and venture out into the world on your own. Either that, or you had to make your way to college or start working at a job in another state, and it was more like, "Ready or not, here you go!"

Either way, you are faced with some major life decisions at the moment that include deciding on whether you should rent or buy a house.

Buying a house is a long-term commitment, but depending on your situation, it could be the right option. However, renting is typically the first experience for newly independent adults. But let us consider closely what the best decision is for you at different points that you may be in life.

Renting or Owning

Whichever option you decide to go with, it is important to know that the answer is entirely dependent on you, your choices and goals, and your financial stability. If you want to buy a home but you can't afford it, then renting a home or apartment may be a better option.

When you consider that buying or renting a home is not the only financial expense you may have, you may need to consider if you would still be able to afford to live and survive while paying the cost of rent or paying off a home loan.

In some cases, you could look at the same exact property, and renting it may cost more than buying it because you are incurring maintenance costs (that you don't have to physically carry out but that you need to pay someone else to do), and perhaps the rental company adds on their extra share. Each choice has its pros and cons (Majaski, 2019):

- The biggest benefit that comes with both renting a home and owning a home is that, either way, you will have a place to lay your head at night and sleep. This is one of the smaller blessings that gets overlooked, but any place that you can call your own, no matter what the size is, knowing you can sleep peacefully and safely is a great accomplishment.

- While renting a home often means that you have a landlord or a caretaker to handle all maintenance needs, owning a home means that you have to take care of repairs, paint jobs, lighting changes, and every other problem you may encounter in your home. You have a greater responsibility when it is your own home, and this comes with the added cost of taxes and things that you don't think about like trash, pest control, home insurance, lawn care, and even pool maintenance.

- While owning a home does give you a unique sense of pride, it doesn't mean that renting is a waste of money. They both serve specific purposes that can meet you at whichever financial state you find yourself in. Both require you to be financially stable, and both give you a great sense of responsibility.

- If you expect your current living situation to change within the next two to three years, which it might, especially if you are going off to college, then you may want to consider renting instead of buying a home.

Buying a Car

Now that you've hopefully got your living arrangements sorted out, it's time to get yourself a pair of reliable wheels to get you to and from everywhere you need to be. Your first option, which may be viable should the opportunity present itself, is to gladly take a hand-me-down car that your parents or older siblings are willing to give you. This is great for two reasons: First, they are not going to give you a car that is unreliable or that they haven't properly taken care of, and second, having a secondhand car is an absolute blessing. If your car works and you can afford to put gas in it, you're already winning in life.

Much like buying or renting a home, there are many things to consider when it comes to buying a car, one of which is whether or not you can afford it. If you can't afford it, it may be wise to look at public transport or lift sharing options.

If you are working and you are in a position to consider buying a car, you may need to think about buying a used vehicle or about buying a car that is more beneficial for practical use rather than for look or status appeal.

When you're considering buying a car, there are a few options to think about:

1. You could lease a car, which is where you pay a fixed amount to use a car for a certain period of time. You could lease a car on a short-term or a long-term basis, but you never truly get to own the car you are driving.

2. You could take out a loan to buy a car. This is one of the most commonly used methods to buy a car, and in these cases, you get the loan from a bank or a financial institution and then pay the loan back with interest. This does mean that the bank or financial institute will own your vehicle until your financial debt is settled with them. Dealerships also offer loans, but usually you can get a better rate from your bank.

3. Lastly, remember that money you started saving up when you were 13? Maybe you have saved enough up to buy your very own car. This is probably the best option when it comes to buying a car, but it is not always a realistic option. Nevertheless, if you are in a position to buy a vehicle for yourself, that is the option that you could pursue.

Now that you have your own space and your own wheels and know how to properly take care of and maintain these aspects of your life, it is time to learn how to take care of yourself and keep yourself and your space safe.

Chapter 6: Safety

The danger which is least expected soonest comes to us. –
Voltaire

"That will never happen to me." How often have you said that
or even thought that when you heard of an unfortunate incident
occurring? We live in a scary world, and this is not where the
horror part of the story begins, just the serious part that we often
ignore or take for granted.

You see, safety is an important part of life and cannot be
ignored. We are under the false impression that bad things
happen around us but never to us. While it is great to live life
with little to no fear, we still need to be cautious, having an
understanding of safety practices even if we never need to use
them.

Health Care

A starting point for safety is knowing what to do when you
aren't feeling too great. This can be when you are sick with a

cold or flu, or it can be in case of an emergency if you have been in an accident.

If it is a case of an emergency, chances are, you or someone else would immediately call for help. However, once the initial state of shock has calmed down, and even after you have gone home, you need to keep and eye on certain things such as bruising appearing from nowhere (as this could be a sign of internal bleeding) and coughing up blood, hallucinating, or having difficulty remembering (as this can be a sign of a concussion).

If you find yourself sick with a cold or with the flu, you may not even notice yourself getting progressively worse. It is important to keep an eye on your symptoms so that you know when to head to the doctor or the emergency room, especially if you are alone.

In most cases, a cold or flu can be treated through self-medication that you can obtain without a prescription from your local pharmacy. Based on your symptoms, the pharmacist will provide you with treatment for each symptom, along with doses and a guide for how often you should take the medication. After a week at the most, you should begin feeling better.

However, during this time, it is important to eat well, drink plenty of liquids, and have a thermometer on hand so that you can monitor your temperature. When your body is actively fighting a virus or infection, your temperature increases. This is because most viruses or bacteria can't survive in high temperatures (NHS, 2022a). Basically, a fever is a good sign that your body is doing what it needs to, but just as viruses and bacteria can't survive in excessively high temperatures, your body may also begin buckling under the strain of the heat caused by your immune system.

If your fever goes too high and is above 105 °F, it can negatively affect your health. You may find yourself having hallucinations, feeling disorientated, or drifting in and out of consciousness. In addition, your breathing can be adversely affected, and you may even experience seizures (Duda, 2022).

In this case, if your fever is really high and it stays high for more than a few hours, you need to seek medical attention as soon as possible.

Taking care of your health isn't only important when you are sick, but it requires your care and attention always. Make sure you do certain things to take preventative measures against getting sick. This can involve things like taking daily vitamins and supplements, eating healthy meals, sanitizing your hands, and making sure you don't place yourself in a position to make others sick if you are feeling under the weather.

Physical Attacks

We know how scary the world can be. Some may say it is more scary if you are a girl. Knowing how to keep yourself safe and knowing what to do if you do find yourself in danger can be the line between staying alive and not staying alive.

Here are some tips that you can use for physical safety (Desoto County Sheriff's Office, n.d.):

- Wherever you are and wherever you go, always stay alert to your surroundings and be aware of what is going on around you. Avoid using earbuds or headphones when you are alone, and try to keep your cell phone in your pocket (ready to dial 911 if you are feeling unsettled).

- It is not always realistic to head to the store with an entourage of people, so make sure that you park in a well-lit area, keep your eyes on everything that is happening around you, and keep a weapon in your hands at all times, whether it is a taser, pepper spray, or something to poke someone in the eyes.

- Try to avoid potentially dangerous situations. Before you unlock and leave your vehicle, check the surrounding areas of the place you are about to enter. Does it seem like any suspicious people are walking around, do you foresee a possible situation that may make you the subject of harassment, or do you feel generally unsafe in your location? If that is the case, always trust your gut.

- Lock your doors immediately to prevent intruders from entering.

- Don't publicly share your location if you are heading out, and always be sure to pour your own drinks.

- If the opportunity to take a self-defense class presents itself, take the course. It may save your life or someone else's life some day.

Sometimes, despite the efforts and attempts that you have made to prevent yourself from being a victim of physical attacks, you may still find yourself or someone else in an unfortunate situation.

If you are physically attacked, the first thing you need to do is call the police. You are going to want to make sure that they come to the exact location where you are. If you are alone, ask someone to wait with you, especially if they have witnessed the incident. Additionally, you're going to want to stay in the same clothes that you were in when the attack took place. As strange as it may be, you are covered in evidence, and it will allow the police to help you build a case against an assailant. Try not to cover yourself with a jacket or blanket until the police come, and be sure to let the emergency responders know if you need an ambulance as well.

They will treat you and take care of you while making sure they do whatever they need to do to find the person who has attacked you.

Once you have been treated for the physical trauma you may have experienced, you need to overcome the mental trauma that you will face after such an incident. But the mental aspect of such incidents are often overlooked. It is important to take care of your mind and your heart and allow yourself to heal from the repetitive thoughts that may flood your thoughts.

The first thing you need to do is fully accept and acknowledge your emotions. There is no need to deny what you are feeling or pretend to be fine. Find people who will support your feelings of not being fine and take rest in the comfort that you are processing all the emotions you are feeling.

Pay attention to your thoughts at this time also. It is easy to get caught up in the negativity of the incident. Remind yourself that you are still alive and protect your mind while you can.

Utilize any resources that are available to you from professional services to your friends and community that are around you.

Also, be compassionate to yourself. In many cases, victims tend to blame themselves, but that is neither realistic, nor true, nor fair.

Physical and Cybersafety

When you think of physical safety, perhaps all that comes to mind is carrying pepper spray or some form of self-defense weapon. But you may consider other tips when taking into account your safety, such as avoiding tying your hair in a ponytail or a bun, staying with friends wherever possible, and being safe when using lift-sharing services.

One great way of staying safe when using an Uber or a Lyft when you're alone is to phone someone who is expecting you at your destination. Make the phone call in front of the driver so that they are aware that someone is expecting you. Give them all the trip-related details, such as where you are currently being picked up from, what is the estimated arrival time at the destination, and the details of the car in which you are in. You can also share your live location preferably with your family or friend groups on social media so that they can track where you are at any moment.

Additionally, when it comes to cybersafety, you need to be cautious and take care not to share sensitive information with anyone online. People are always coming up with new ways to steal your information and money so you need to make sure that you have the basics covered and stay up-to-date with the new methods criminals may come up with.

First and foremost, when it comes to digital safety, you need to keep your passwords safe and secure. I think it goes without saying that having one password for everything is not a great idea. However, there are many digital platforms, including Google, that will keep track of your passwords so you don't have to, and they keep those passwords secure. You can also make sure to use biometric access points where the options are available so that no one gets into your digital space but you.

If you make a bank transfer, know who the recipient is. There are many schemes to separate you from your money. Remember, no one ever needs you to send them money so that they can send you money, and if it sounds too good to be true, it probably is.

Once you know that you are safe, you can begin living in your most natural space. You see, many generations before, you never had a guidebook or a handbook on the preparation needed to thrive in the outside world. So consider yourself as already having an upper hand. But you will quickly find yourself following a natural flow that makes all the "you musts" and "you shoulds" seem like an absolutely natural and normal part of life.

Once you have this in place, it is time to work on yourself and your own personal development.

First Aid

One of the first things you need to do when you move into your own home is make sure you have a first aid kit and a fire extinguisher. Having these two items are important in case of an emergency.

For the most part, your first aid kit would need to contain some of these items (NHS Choices, 2019):

- bandages and gauze dressing to treat wounds

- sterilizing ointment or rubbing alcohol

- plasters

- scissors

- safety pins and tweezers

- antihistamine medication

- distilled water or a solution to clean wounds

- antibiotic ointment

- painkillers

When you are living on your own, it is your responsibility to make sure that your first aid kit is always adequately stocked for any emergency. Additionally, if the opportunity to take any first aid courses presents itself, such as CPR courses, you should consider taking it. It can save a life.

Other emergency skills that will prove helpful to know are (Ryser, 2019):

1. How to do abdominal thrusts in case of choking. To do this, you need to stand behind someone who is choking, ball your hands into fists and place it under their rib cage. Then you're going to thrust upwards into the cavity beneath their rib cage until whatever they are choking on dislodges.

2. If someone gets an injury that leads to excessive bleeding, you need to apply firm pressure to the wound until the bleeding stops. Even once help arrives, you want to keep applying pressure until medical professionals take over.

3. If someone sustains a burn, apply a topical burn cream to the area or run it under cool water. If the burn is excessively bad and you are nervous about treating it, you should immediately take the person to the emergency room for doctors to treat the area and to prevent infection from setting in.

4. You should learn how to make a splint in case of a broken bone. To do this, you're going to need two pieces of wood or other sturdy support and a large piece of material, whether it is clothing or something else to tie. You want to make sure you don't move the bone from its current position, and if a bone is protruding, you should make a donut shape out of another piece of material so the bone is placed in the hole and doesn't get forced downward or moved by the splint.

5. If someone hits their head or has a fall, you should keep an eye out for a concussion. You should also be able to notice if someone is acting strangely or out of the ordinary. They may throw up or be dizzy, and they may not make sense when they speak. Additionally, you should be able to spot if someone is having a stroke by asking them to place their arms in the air, to speak, and to smile. If they have any difficulties or irregularities in doing these tasks, get to the hospital immediately.

Chapter 7: Personal Development

When it is obvious that the goals cannot be reached, don't adjust the goals, adjust the action steps. –Confucius

Many people think that once they have a home and a car, then they have made a success of themselves. But success isn't measured by what you have but rather on who you are and how you manage and handle what you have. There is no point having the most beautiful home but nothing that you are working toward and no personal development goals you are hoping to achieve.

Setting Goals

You may think that you have accomplished everything you need to in life, but because we are constantly moving and adapting as individuals, it is important to revisit the goals we have accomplished and set new goals for ourselves as we reach new milestones in life. This keeps us progressing and keeps giving us something to look forward to.

For example, if you have a holiday planned for three months from now, it is somewhat of a goal you have set and achieved for yourself, but also a goal you need to achieve. You see, you would have needed to work hard and put in extra effort to be able to afford the holiday. You would also need to complete certain tasks before you actually go on your vacation, which means that you have set a holiday goal for yourself.

It doesn't always need to be goals that look like holidays or vacations, but it could be working hard to earn a new skill, placing a deadline on yourself, or setting financial goals. Once you achieve your goals, that is not the end of the road. Then, it is time to revisit the goal, set new ones, and start again.

How to Set Goals

Setting goals isn't just about writing them down on a piece of paper and hoping these dreams and wishes come to pass. It takes hard work and effort to achieve those goals. When you set a goal, you are not putting an end goal down; instead, you are going to write down the details of how you are going to achieve this goal as well. This makes sure that it isn't just a destination, but a journey instead.

So how do you set goals? Well, some top tips that I can give you before telling you how to set goals is first, don't just write down the goal, but write down *how* you're going to achieve the goal as well. This will make sure you are invested in the entire process, and if you don't achieve your goal, you can go back and look at why.

The next tip that I can give you is to constantly reassess your goals. Write it down and make it concrete. Put it where you can see it often, so you can constantly look at it and be reminded of what you want in life.

And the last tip is to always attach a date to the goal. A goal without a deadline is something that has the potential to stay in the pipeline.

Now, how do you set a goal? Here are some tips (Eastern Washington University, n.d.):

- When you set goals, think of the now and of the future, and set goals for both. Set smaller short-term goals that can be milestones leading up to the bigger long-term goal, or they can be entirely unrelated to your long-term goal and they can be things you can achieve faster.

- Try to set SMART goals. These are specific, measurable, attainable, relevant, and time-based.

- Your goals should be things that are going to motivate you to be better. They are going to move you from your current point to a higher point.

- Make your goals tangible by putting them on paper and making them easy to see.

- As you grow and change as a person, your goals need to change too. Maybe your goal is to get a job abroad, but you meet someone and you form a romantic attachment with them and you decide that you would like to get a job closer to them. This goal is going to be adjusted.

- Last, you're going to give yourself credit when it's due, you're going to applaud your achievements, and you're going to reward yourself when necessary. This will push you to keep going on.

Habits

You are the culmination of all your habits. Everything you do on a daily basis makes you the person you are. If you form healthy habits, you will be a healthy person. If you form a habit of being someone who brings others down, that's who you will become and you will find those people spending less and less time with you.

Habits are behaviors that are repeated. They can be things that you are aware and conscious of, or they can be things that happen almost automatically with little to no thought.

Forming healthy habits is in line with setting goals. Healthy habits are what help you achieve your goals. But forming habits is neither easy nor quick, but everyone has the capability of setting healthy goals.

When you create healthy habits, it helps you think of and prepare for the future.

Time Management

Taking care of your time is something that is overlooked. How many times have you thought that it's okay if you're late as long as you have told the person waiting that you're going to be late? If you are able to manage your time, you will be able to show up on time because when you are late, you give people the impression that their time doesn't matter to you.

Here are some important time management skills that you could use in your life:

- plan what you need to do in a specific time

- make a time sensitive list of what needs to be done and when it needs to be done

- prioritize tasks in terms of urgency

- be realistic about the time you need to do a task

Problem-Solving

There are many ways to determine whether or not you're going to thrive in this world. One way that will impact how you succeed is the way you approach and deal with problems. As you grow and mature, you realize there is more than one way to approach a situation and that the best solution in some cases may be speed and, in others, it may be accuracy.

Also, the types of problems that you are going to face are going to differ greatly in life. When you're in high school, your biggest problems may be tests and exams. When you get older, you may have financial concerns, but the way you solve these problems will ultimately determine your success because, well, you either did a good job, or you didn't.

Before you dive head first into solving a problem, it's important to develop a game plan. The last thing you want to do is dive head first into problem-solving and end up doing it poorly twice instead of right once.

When you have a plan in place, it is always a good idea to get a second opinion. Sometimes, you may be too close to the situation and may need to step away and let someone with a fresh perspective provide you with an opinion that you may not have thought of.

Finally, it is time to execute your plan. The important thing that you need to remember in this process of problem-solving is that whether or not your plan works, you need to either learn from the mistake and adapt, or you can count this as a success. In

each circumstance, you need to learn and you need to adapt—
that is how you thrive.

Conclusion

When I began writing this book, I had an intention in mind to pass along the valuable skills that most teens need but are never taught. There is no blame on anyone for not teaching you these things. The norm of this world is that you get thrust into a new environment and you learn on the go, you adapt and hopefully find your feet before you fall over.

But, as someone who has faced this, who has seen others struggle, my intention is to prepare as many people as possible for what is about to come their way in a life they are so greatly anticipating.

The reason is simple: Why not? If I know the why and the how, why wouldn't I want to share it with someone else?

With that being said, this book is filled with skills and tips that you need to thrive when you reach certain milestones in your life. Whether you find yourself in need of every piece of advice in this book or whether one point has resounded through and that is the one thing you have taken away from this book, well then, reader, I have done my job.

The purpose of this book was never to overwhelm you and bombard you with information you will never use. Instead, it is information that is secured in your treasure chest so should you find yourself or someone else needing this information, you have it.

As I said, it is better to have it and not need it, than need it and not have it.

Now spread your wings, and go live your most fruitful life!

Thank you so much for supporting my dream as an independent author. Your decision to purchase and read my book means everything to me! I couldn't have made it this far without amazing readers like you!

As you know, reviews are crucial for independent authors like me to reach a wider audience and continue pursuing our passion.

I would greatly appreciate it if you could leave an honest review on Amazon by scanning the QR code below or going to the link below.

obiez.com/reviewlifeskillsgirls

References

Adobe. (n.d.) How to keep important documents safe https://www.adobe.com/acrobat/resources/keep-documents-safe-in-a-disaster.html

Allie. (2016, November 1). *20 inspiring quotes on health, life & balance.* OmBody Health. https://ombodyhealth.com/20-inspiring-quotes-health-life-balance/

Arm & Hammer. (n.d.). *7 easy & efficient laundry tips & tricks.* https://www.armandhammer.com/articles/laundry-tips-hacks

Asana. (2022). *6 steps to create a daily schedule template.* https://asana.com/resources/daily-schedule-template

Avendano, K. (2022, April 29). 40 inspirational mental health quotes. *Good Housekeeping.* https://www.goodhousekeeping.com/life/a39739060/mental-health-quotes/

Bank of America. (2019). *Creating a budget with a personal budget spreadsheet.* Better Money Habits. https://bettermoneyhabits.bankofamerica.com/en/saving-budgeting/creating-a-budget

Bhandari, S. (2016, December 13). *What does stress do to the body?* WebMD. https://www.webmd.com/balance/stress-management/stress-and-the-body

Brill & Rinaldi. (n.d.). *Five steps to take immediately after an auto accident.* https://www.forpeopleforjustice.com/five-steps-to-take-immediately-after-an-auto-accident/

British Heart Foundation. (2015). *The most common excuses to avoid exercise (and how to beat them).* https://www.bhf.org.uk/informationsupport/heart-matters-magazine/wellbeing/ditch-the-excuses

Canada Drives. (n.d.). *Car maintenance checklist: 9 essential steps that anyone can do.* https://www.canadadrives.ca/blog/maintenance/car-maintenance-checklist-essentials

Centers for Disease Control and Prevention. (2016). *Sleep hygiene tips - sleep and sleep disorders.* https://www.cdc.gov/sleep/about_sleep/sleep_hygiene.html

Centers for Disease Control and Prevention. (2018). *Learn about mental health - mental health.* Www.cdc.gov. https://www.cdc.gov/mentalhealth/learn/index.htm

Centers for Disease Control and Prevention. (2022a, April 27). *Benefits of physical activity.* https://www.cdc.gov/physicalactivity/basics/pa-health/index.htm

Centers for Disease Control and Prevention. (2022b, July 14). *Personal hygiene.* https://www.cdc.gov/hygiene/personal-hygiene/index.html

Centers for Disease Control and Prevention. (2022c, December 1). *Menstrual hygiene.* https://www.cdc.gov/hygiene/personal-hygiene/menstrual.html

Chatel, A. (2015). *17 first date etiquette rules everyone should follow (none of which involve being proper).* Bustle. https://www.bustle.com/articles/66742-17-first-date-etiquette-rules-everyone-should-follow-none-of-which-involve-being-proper

Cjco. (2020, January 19). *Finding the "right" person in relationships.* Courage to Connect Counseling. https://www.courage2connect.com/finding-the-right-person-in-relationships/

Coursera. (2022, August 17). *What is effective communication? Skills for work, school, and life.* https://www.coursera.org/articles/communication-effectiveness

Desoto County Sheriff's Office. (n.d.). *Tips for women on staying safe.* https://www.desotosheriff.com/community/tips_for_women_on_staying_safe!.php

Deutschendorf, H. (2015, February 2). 7 key habits for building better relationships. *Fast Company.*

https://www.fastcompany.com/3041774/7-key-habits-for-building-better-relationships

Direct Energy. (n.d.). *How can I prepare my home for a flood?* https://www.directenergy.com/learning-center/prepare-home-flood

Doan, D. (2023). *Entrepreneurship vs. employment — the complete list of pros and cons.* Hubspot. https://blog.hubspot.com/sales/entrepreneurship-vs-employment

Duda, K. (2022). *When is a fever too high?* Verywell Health. https://www.verywellhealth.com/when-is-a-fever-too-high-770347

Eastern Washington University. (n.d.). *Goal-Setting.* https://inside.ewu.edu/calelearning/psychological-skills/goal-setting/

Fann-Im, N. (2021, February 12). *How to prepare for a flood.* This Old House. https://www.thisoldhouse.com/natural-disasters/22275081/preparing-for-a-flood

Friedman, K. (2022). *25 quick and easy tips for organizing your entire kitchen.* HGTV. https://www.hgtv.com/lifestyle/clean-and-organize/quick-easy-kitchen-organization-ideas

Garfield, S. (2019, October 15). *What are the qualities of good communicators?* Medium. https://stangarfield.medium.com/what-are-the-qualities-of-good-communicators-23c9fa773ef8

Goldman, L. (2019, November 22). *Depression: What it is, symptoms, causes, treatment, types, and more.* Medical News Today. https://www.medicalnewstoday.com/articles/8933

Goodreads. (n.d.). *A quote by Dalai Lama XIV.* https://www.goodreads.com/quotes/31335-we-human-beings-are-social-beings-we-come-into-the

Indeed. (2021). *70+ motivational quotes about achieving goals.* Indeed Career Guide. https://www.indeed.com/career-advice/career-development/achieving-goals-quotes

Kiander, T. (2012, October 17). *How to create a to-do list that super boosts your productivity.* Lifehack. https://www.lifehack.org/articles/productivity/how-to-create-a-to-do-list-that-makes-you-smile.html#how-to-create-a-to-do-list-that-works-for-you

Kidscape. (n.d.). *How to make new friends.* https://www.kidscape.org.uk/advice/advice-for-young-people/friendships-and-frenemies/how-to-make-new-friends/

Kohyama, J. (2021). Which is more important for health: Sleep quantity or sleep quality? *Children, 8*(7), 542. https://doi.org/10.3390/children8070542

Lanquist, L. (2021). *Neat freaks, rejoice: Here is the ultimate guide to organizing your house.* MyDomaine. https://www.mydomaine.com/how-to-organize-your-house-5203629

Larkin, E. (2020, October 25). *How to create a daily routine that works for you.* The Spruce. https://www.thespruce.com/how-to-create-a-daily-routine-2648007

Law Insider. (n.d.). *Living space definition.* https://www.lawinsider.com/dictionary/living-space

Lifford, J. (2020, February 13). *How to organize your kitchen.* Clean and Scentsible. https://www.cleanandscentsible.com/8-steps-to-an-organized-kitchen-february-hod/

Lyness, D. (2018). *Dealing with peer pressure (for kids).* Kids Health. https://kidshealth.org/en/kids/peer-pressure.html

Majaski, C. (2019). *The difference between renting and owning a home.* Investopedia. https://www.investopedia.com/articles/personal-finance/083115/renting-vs-owning-home-pros-and-cons.asp

Martins, J. (2022). *Revamp your to-do list with these 15 tips.* Asana. https://asana.com/resources/make-better-to-do-lists

MasterClass. (2021). *How to organize kitchen cabinets: 10 organization tips.* https://www.masterclass.com/articles/how-to-organize-kitchen-cabinets

Mayo Clinic. (2021, October 8). *7 great reasons why exercise matters.* https://www.mayoclinic.org/healthy-lifestyle/fitness/in-depth/exercise/art-20048389

McRae, L. (2019, September 25). *How to start a new routine and stick to it,* Northshore. https://www.northshore.org/healthy-you/how-to-start-a-new-routine-and-stick-to-it/

Mercy Care. (2022). *Health benefits of social interaction.*https://www.mercycare.org/bhs/employee-assistance-program/eapforemployers/resources/health-benefits-of-social-interaction/

Michaels, D. (2020, August 11). *How to stock a pantry for the first time on a budget.* From This Kitchen Table. https://www.fromthiskitchentable.com/how-to-stock-a-pantry-for-the-first-time/

Mind Tools. (n.d.). *Making a great first impression.* Www.mindtools.com. https://www.mindtools.com/a391uhu/making-a-great-first-impression

Mindful. (2019, April 13). *How to meditate.* https://www.mindful.org/how-to-meditate/

Nast, C. (2018, October 22). 16 living room organization tips we swear by. *Architectural Digest.* https://www.architecturaldigest.com/story/living-room-organization-tips-we-swear-by

National Heart, Lung, and Blood Institute. (2022, March 24). *How sleep works - why is sleep important?* National Institutes of Health. https://www.nhlbi.nih.gov/health/sleep/why-sleep-important

Nationwide Children's Hospital. (n.d.). *Cooking safety.* https://www.nationwidechildrens.org/research/areas-of-research/center-for-injury-research-and-policy/injury-topics/home-safety/cooking-safety

Neason, A. (2022, May 1). *How to organize a living room — 10 tips and tricks from professional organizers and interior designers.* Living Etc. https://www.livingetc.com/advice/how-to-organize-a-living-room

NHS. (2022a). *Fever in adults.* https://www.nhsinform.scot/illnesses-and-conditions/infections-and-poisoning/fever-in-adults

NHS. (2022b, February 24). *8 tips for healthy eating.* https://www.nhs.uk/live-well/eat-well/how-to-eat-a-balanced-diet/eight-tips-for-healthy-eating/

NHS Choices. (2019). *What should I keep in my first aid kit?* https://www.nhs.uk/common-health-questions/accidents-first-aid-and-treatments/what-should-i-keep-in-my-first-aid-kit/

National Institutes of Health. (2018, November 1). *Creating healthy habits.* NIH News in Health. https://newsinhealth.nih.gov/2018/03/creating-healthy-habits

Northwestern Medicine. (2022). *Health benefits of having a routine.* https://www.nm.org/healthbeat/healthy-tips/health-benefits-of-having-a-routine

Personal-Finance. (2019, May 30). *What are investment assets?* Financial Security for All. https://personal-finance.extension.org/what-are-investment-assets/

Pous, T. (2017). *12 rules for making plans with friends like a grown-ass adult.* BuzzFeed. https://www.buzzfeed.com/terripous/12-rules-for-making-plans-with-friends-like-a-grown-ass-adul

RAC. (2020). *How to change a tyre in 10 simple steps.* https://www.rac.co.uk/drive/advice/car-maintenance/how-to-change-a-tyre/

Rathner, S. (2020). *Starter credit card options: Student card or secured card?* NerdWallet. https://www.nerdwallet.com/article/credit-cards/starter-credit-card-student-card-vs-secured-card

Raypole, C. (2019, November 13). *Extroverts, introverts, and everything in between.* Healthline. https://www.healthline.com/health/extrovert-vs-introvert

Ready.gov. (2017). *Power outages.* https://www.ready.gov/power-outages

Richards, L. (2022, May 6). *What is driving anxiety? Causes, symptoms, and treatment.* Medical News Today. https://www.medicalnewstoday.com/articles/driving-anxiety

Riopel, L. (2019, June 14). *The importance, benefits, and value of goal setting.* Positive Psychology. https://positivepsychology.com/benefits-goal-setting/

Ryser, S. (2019). *Basic first aid skills everyone should learn.* Idaho Medical Academy. https://www.idahomedicalacademy.com/basic-first-aid-skills-everyone-should-learn/

Santaella, E. (2021, January 21). *Eye-level is buy level — the principles of visual merchandising.* Mobile Insight. https://mobileinsight.com/eye-level-buy-level-importance-store-product-placement/

Seitz, A. (2021, November 2). *25 simple tips to make your diet healthier.* Healthline. https://www.healthline.com/nutrition/healthy-eating-tips#

Shaffer, J. (2017, December 8). Top 10 kitchen safety do's and don'ts. *Taste of Home.* https://www.tasteofhome.com/article/kitchen-safety-tips/

Skilled at Life. (2016, May 27). *18 reasons why a daily routine is so important.* https://www.skilledatlife.com/18-reasons-why-a-daily-routine-is-so-important/

Suni, E. (2020, December 17). *Sleep quality: How to determine if you're getting poor sleep.* Sleep Foundation. https://www.sleepfoundation.org/sleep-hygiene/how-to-determine-poor-quality-sleep

TJ Woods Insurance Agency, Inc. (2013). *Top kitchen safety tips.* https://woodsinsurance.com/top-kitchen-safety-tips/

Walden University. (2021). *How to be an effective communicator in 7 easy steps.* https://www.waldenu.edu/programs/communication/resource/how-to-be-an-effective-communicator-in-7-easy-steps

Water Science School. (2019, May 22). *The water in you: Water and the human body.* U.S. Geological Survey.

https://www.usgs.gov/special-topics/water-science-school/science/water-you-water-and-human-body

WikiHow. (2007, June 18). *Get your driver's license in the USA.* https://www.wikihow.com/Get-Your-Driver%27s-License-in-the-USA

Winke, R. (2021, June 30). *How to organize and store important documents at home.* Family Handyman. https://www.familyhandyman.com/article/document-storage/

Wrinkle Free Delivery. (2021, May 5). *How to set color and stop dye bleeding in clothes.* https://wrinklefreedelivery.com/laundry/how-to-set-color-and-stop-dye-bleeding-in-clothes/

Zahair, A. (2021). Why it's important that you keep your home organized. *Build Magazine.* https://www.build-review.com/why-its-important-that-you-keep-your-home-organized/